TEXTILE ❖ BELT ❖ MAKING

Linda P. Schapper

Sterling Publishing Co., Inc.   New York

For golden-haired, nine-year-old Alexa Schaefer, my
guest artist, who took my hand when the sun wouldn't
shine and showed me how to spot baby chameleons on a
familiar tree.

Library of Congress Cataloging-in-Publication Data

Schäpper, Linda.
    Textile belt making.

    Includes index.
    1. Textile crafts. 2. Belts (Clothing)
I. Title.
TT699.S36 1988 746.9′2   88-4845
ISBN 0-8069-6585-1
ISBN 0-8069-6584-3 (pbk.)

1   3   5   7   9   10   8   6   4   2

Copyright © 1988 by Linda Schäpper
Published by Sterling Publishing Co., Inc.
Two Park Avenue, New York, N.Y. 10016
Distributed in Canada by Oak Tree Press Ltd.
% Canadian Manda Group. P.O. Box 920, Station U
Toronto, Ontario, Canada M8Z 5P9
Distributed in the United Kingdom by Blandford Press
Link House, West Street, Poole, Dorset BH15 1LL, England
Distributed in Australia by Capricorn Ltd.
P.O. Box 665, Lane Cove, NSW 2066
Manufactured in the United States of America
All rights reserved

Contents

Introduction

Belts can be fun to make, flattering to wear, and a welcome addition to any wardrobe. They can be used to make a simple dress elegant for evening wear, to make it appear sporty or casual for afternoon wear, or just plain different for those on a limited budget.

Any figure type can wear a belt. Even those who say they don't have a waist would find they had one if they wore belts. There are ways of manipulating the shape and size of the waist by using different colors and designs in the belt.

Belts are too often traditional and utilitarian in materials and design. There are many unexplored possibilities of design through the use of textiles. The use of textiles offers greater versatility in color, texture and techniques. The same pattern would look completely different if one used small cotton prints or glittery gold or silver. The same material looks very different if lined and quilted, or cut and then reassembled by the use of small patches. Many of the techniques I have chosen are more commonly associated with other products.

Crochet is usually used for sweaters or blankets. Patchwork and quilting would normally be thought of for large bedspreads. Folding and cut out work would normally be used more in paper arts.

Textile belts are easy to make and don't require a lot of time. They require little material and can be made, using one technique or a combination of several. They can be adapted for any age group or any occasion merely by changing the use of fabric and design. One reason they're so easy to make is that the only pattern requirement is to know the length and width of the belt. As you grow in experience and self-confidence, more difficult and time-consuming techniques can be used.

I hope to suggest ideas for your own patterns. This book should be used as a catalyst in your designing rather than as a definitive pattern book. I will describe shapes, color possibilities, and techniques. You as the artist must take it from there and adapt these concepts to your own personal style and taste.

METRIC EQUIVALENCY CHART

MM—MILLIMETRES   CM—CENTIMETRES

INCHES TO MILLIMETRES AND CENTIMETRES

INCHES	MM	CM	INCHES	CM	INCHES	CM
⅛	3	0.3	9	22.9	30	76.2
¼	6	0.6	10	25.4	31	78.7
⅜	10	1.0	11	27.9	32	81.3
½	13	1.3	12	30.5	33	83.8
⅝	16	1.6	13	33.0	34	86.4
¾	19	1.9	14	35.6	35	88.9
⅞	22	2.2	15	38.1	36	91.4
1	25	2.5	16	40.6	37	94.0
1¼	32	3.2	17	43.2	38	96.5
1½	38	3.8	18	45.7	39	99.1
1¾	44	4.4	19	48.3	40	101.6
2	51	5.1	20	50.8	41	104.1
2½	64	6.4	21	53.3	42	106.7
3	76	7.6	22	55.9	43	109.2
3½	89	8.9	23	58.4	44	111.8
4	102	10.2	24	61.0	45	114.3
4½	114	11.4	25	63.5	46	116.8
5	127	12.7	26	66.0	47	119.4
6	152	15.2	27	68.6	48	121.9
7	178	17.8	28	71.1	49	124.5
8	203	20.3	29	73.7	50	127.0

YARDS TO METRES

YARDS	METRES	YARDS	METRES	YARDS	METRES	YARDS	METRES	YARDS	METRES
⅛	0.11	2⅛	1.94	4⅛	3.77	6⅛	5.60	8⅛	7.43
¼	0.23	2¼	2.06	4¼	3.89	6¼	5.72	8¼	7.54
⅜	0.34	2⅜	2.17	4⅜	4.00	6⅜	5.83	8⅜	7.66
½	0.46	2½	2.29	4½	4.11	6½	5.94	8½	7.77
⅝	0.57	2⅝	2.40	4⅝	4.23	6⅝	6.06	8⅝	7.89
¾	0.69	2¾	2.51	4¾	4.34	6¾	6.17	8¾	8.00
⅞	0.80	2⅞	2.63	4⅞	4.46	6⅞	6.29	8⅞	8.12
1	0.91	3	2.74	5	4.57	7	6.40	9	8.23
1⅛	1.03	3⅛	2.86	5⅛	4.69	7⅛	6.52	9⅛	8.34
1¼	1.14	3¼	2.97	5¼	4.80	7¼	6.63	9¼	8.46
1⅜	1.26	3⅜	3.09	5⅜	4.91	7⅜	6.74	9⅜	8.57
1½	1.37	3½	3.20	5½	5.03	7½	6.86	9½	8.69
1⅝	1.49	3⅝	3.31	5⅝	5.14	7⅝	6.97	9⅝	8.80
1¾	1.60	3¾	3.43	5¾	5.26	7¾	7.09	9¾	8.92
1⅞	1.71	3⅞	3.54	5⅞	5.37	7⅞	7.20	9⅞	9.03
2	1.83	4	3.66	6	5.49	8	7.32	10	9.14

BASICS

Creativity

Everyone is creative. One of the saddest things is to hear someone say that he or she is not creative. Often that has resulted from an art teacher who criticized too harshly way back as far as the first grade, or strict parents, or a difficult relationship.

Creativity is the same as sensitivity. It's the feeling of authority to take things and put them together in a way we like—the feeling that we have the *right* to select things to be the way we want them. My first love is primitive, more often called "naive," painting. When I lived in Beirut there seemed to be only grief and death everywhere and, after several months of bombing, it was all I could paint. But I didn't want to focus on the sadness and wound up painting happy, bright-eyed people walking to the cemetery amidst beautiful valleys and flowering trees. I painted things the way I wanted to see them.

We all have our own unique way of interpreting everything we see and feel. There are over 400 different shades of the color red. If the same red was shown to different people, few would agree on which red they saw. Descriptions given to the police at the scene of a crime are often so different there is no common thread. Each person sees a different set of circumstances. Experiments in counselling situations will require one person to say something about the way he feels. The other person is supposed to paraphrase what was said. They are often required to repeat the exercise four or five times until they can hear and understand exactly what is said. We are all different and it's all right to be different. Why not put these differences to good use?

Start questioning everything. Discard all the rules. Somebody else made the rules. Why should you accept them without thinking them through and deciding for yourself? Fashion is always changing. What is "in" one year is "out" the next. When I was in school, it was considered bad taste to put blue and green together, or red and pink. Then these combinations came into fashion. After a while they became so common, they stopped being used. Use colors in unusual ways. Use textures other than for their normal use. Use materials in unexpected ways. Denim is thought of as rough and ready and sporty. Embellish it with gold or silver lamé, embroider it and see how different it can look. Try different shapes. Perhaps some of your ideas will turn out to be mistakes. Don't worry. Everybody makes them.

Experts say that an artist will be satisfied with 1 out of 10 of his or her paintings. A photographer will be happy with one excellent shot in a roll of 36. The aim should be to learn by your mistakes. Learn about your own tastes. Learn what you like and what you don't. Learn what style and type of design will suit you best. Learn about colors. Learn that the only way not to make a mistake is to do nothing. Taking a risk is part of any creative venture.

Years ago, I did research into why certain creative women were successful and others not. I found out that the same types of difficult circumstances and unwelcome surprises happen to them as to people who have not succeeded to the same extent. The difference is that they always seem to get up, dust themselves off and start again. We have to be able to do the same thing.

Starting

The most difficult thing about starting any new project is exactly that: starting. Even after all my years of self-discipline, I still have trouble actually sitting down to start something new. I may have drawn it and designed it and dreamed about it and even need it, but the actual first step is the hardest. At that particular time, all the most undesirable chores seem to take on a new urgency, and I find myself cleaning out the refrigerator, organizing the hall closet, or even washing windows. There always seems to be a nagging fear that I might not be able to do it, that it might not turn out well or that it will somehow fail. The trick is to start. Set aside a time and a place and set a small goal for that first session. It could be a very small goal, perhaps cutting out the pattern or even the basic sewing techniques. Usually, once you have started in any small way the rest will follow.

There are as many ways to start a belt project as there are belts. Sometimes you see a material you like and want to find a way to use it. Sometimes you have an outfit that you would like to supplement or change and you start out looking for an idea for a belt. Perhaps on another occasion you find a pattern you like and look for a way to use it. Or you might want to exercise a new sewing technique, and the small format required for a belt could appeal to you. Any of these ways works and even a combination of them can be a stimulus for an idea. There is no right or wrong way to go about this.

How to get the idea. You can get ideas from anywhere. Once you are on the lookout for ideas you find them literally everywhere. I sometimes compare it to putting a new lens on a camera. You suddenly see things at a whole new angle and perspective. One can get ideas of patterns from flowers, leaves or trees. Look at floor tiles, bricks, lattices. Look at the sky and how the clouds move. Look at animals and at their markings. Once you establish the habit of looking for patterns you will have to learn to shut off your imagination.

Sizing. Sizing is easy. You only have to

decide how wide you want the belt and measure your waist to decide how long. After that just think about how much of an overlap you want—if any. It's easiest to take a small piece of material and cut it to the size and shape you want.

Fitting. A narrow belt is easier to fit to your figure than a wide belt. With a narrow belt you only have to think about the waist or the section where it is to be worn. If it is wide, you have to take into consideration the hips and the curves that it will be covering. It may have to be sculpted to fit the body. This could easily be done by gathering or darts. Play around with sizing. Remember, you are pioneering something new, and there is always risk involved. Take a chance.

Drafting a pattern. I usually begin by sketching an idea. I often color it in with felt pens to get an idea of the color. The next step is to design a scaled-down model to scale. If the finished product is to be 24 inches, I draw a smaller version and play with the proportions at that point. Then if I have questions about the finished design, I can sketch the finished result.

Different shapes possible. A belt can take many different forms. It can wrap around; it can resemble a girdle. It can be sculpted or gathered. I have even stretched the definition to include over-the-shoulder pieces, suspenders and halters. A belt can be anything your imagination wants it to be. (See Illus. 1–9.)

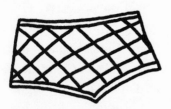

Illus. 1. Band with sash.

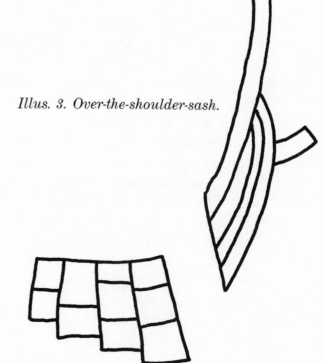

Illus. 3. Over-the-shoulder-sash.

Illus. 2. Girdle.

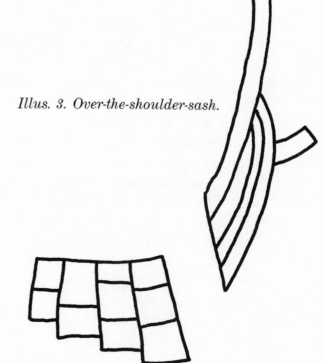

Illus. 4. Staggered girdle.

Attention should be paid to the shape of the body. Some belts are more flattering than others. I like the philosophy of a beautician I knew who would never let the client pick a hair style out of a magazine, because the same style would look very different on each person.

Illus. 5. Tie hip-hugger.

Illus. 6. Cut-outs.

Illus. 7. Straight bands.

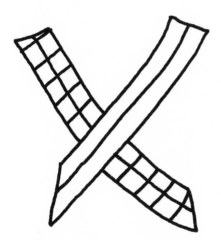

Illus. 8. Double sash.

Illus. 9. Halter belt.

Materials

Any material can be used to make a belt. Leather or some types of synthetic plastic have been used by the commercial fashion industry, but there are almost limitless other possibilities. Silks, satins and even metallics or silver and gold lamé are fun to work with and lend a very expensive air to any belt project.

Take the same design and use corduroys or wools and you have a rich-looking belt suitable for colder climates. Use colorful prints, and they would look good on a child or as warm-weather fashion. Use plain colors that are closely related—for instance, several shades of purple, and you have a strong fashion statement.

The choices can be unusual. I have seen an interesting project, which used clear plastic, enclosing things such as small mementos within the two walls of plastic. Newspaper or foil, even address cards or chewing-gum labels could make an interesting belt. A combination of all the materials could also be used. Wools could be combined with silk or silver lamé. Denim could be combined with lace or printed cotton. There is no limit to what can be done.

Color

Our feelings about color are often subconscious. We see it. It affects us, but we are not always really aware of what colors we like, how they change our moods and often even what color we have been looking at. Color fascinates people. It has the potential of being able to move emotions. You can tell a lot about people from the colors they choose to wear. It is often said that seriously depressed people tend to wear blacks and somber colors.

Certain colors are considered serious or businesslike. If an Englishman were to wear a pink suit to a business conference he would be considered a bit frivolous (to say the least). In different cultures, colors signify different things—even in different time periods. When I was growing up, black and dark colors were the colors of mourning. In India and Sri Lanka, white has been the color of mourning. White has just recently become more acceptable in the United States as a color of mourning. In America, baby girls are often dressed in pink and baby boys in light blue, even though children seem to prefer bright colors.

Our natural surroundings seem to have a lot to do with the colors we choose. I have noticed that Scandinavians love pale colors, whites and beiges. If you travel to Sweden in the winter you can drive miles and miles through fields of snow with light blue sky above and the only color on the ground the golden remains of cattails.

The French seem to love blue and they are surrounded by beautiful blue waters.

In selling bedspreads in the United States it was always possible to sell pastels or any shades of colors on the two coasts, but when you left the coast and got to the middle of the United States they seemed to prefer earth tones. I always thought they were trying to repeat the beautiful browns and beiges of the land surrounding them.

Light has a lot to do with our perception of colors. I have made both clothing and bedspreads in the bright sunlight of India and Sri Lanka and been very disappointed that they were so dull and uninteresting. I then brought them back to the grey light of Europe and have been surprised to take them out of the box and they look completely different. The reverse also happened. I made very bright quilts in India and brought them back to Europe and they were so gaudy I could not look at them.

In Denmark, many clothes are still imported from India and they are comfortable with the color combinations of many shades of purple. In France, these same color combinations would be considered morose. Olive green is a favorite color in Austria and southern Germany where the famous loden coats are very popular. On the other hand, the Swiss rarely wear green, feeling that green is a color of the lush countryside, but not something to wear. I have also been told that the Swiss men spend parts of up to 20 years in the military and the uniform is a familiar sight in Switzerland. It's green and that is also given as a reason why it's not worn.

Magazines and advertisements often influence our taste in colors, although it's an unconscious influence. Every year the fashion industry chooses different color combinations and try to make as much of their line as possible in those colors. Sometimes the colors are the same but the names change. Beige is called "honey" one year, "champignon" the next and "lumber" the next. I watched Paris introduce a color scheme of grey, beige, pumpkin and dull green several years ago. The first unsophisticated reaction was "Yuck, are they kidding, and whoever thought of that?" The next season New York had adopted it and little by little the fashion industry adopted it. Five years later the combination is an accepted staple and I even have to admit to liking it.

I would like to offer some suggestions on how color could be used based on living and working as an artist in several different cultures.

The surprise. One interesting method is to put in a surprise color; one you would not expect. Mix a little pink or apricot in with the browns and beiges. In a mixture of blues, add burgundy or green. Mix in a slight touch of red with beiges and whites. Try a spot of bright yellow with blacks and greys, or a little apple green among somber purples and burgundys.

When planning your colors, map out the colors you really want and then try the opposite color of what you think would go. Almost ask yourself as a joke, "What would be the worst color I could put here," and try it. It might work.

Primary colors. Using the basic colors of red, yellow, blue and green or red, white and blue; or red, yellow and green gives a strong youthful appearance to any design. Several Scandinavian designers have become famous on the basis of their designs in primary colors.

Placing similar shades together. There is something intensely pleasing about placing shades in the same color range together. Work with families of color and around the spectrum to discover which tones please you. Work with shades of reds or purples or blues or greens. Then try to place closely related color together—such as blues and greens or reds and pinks.

If you want to make these shades together more dramatic you could mix them onto a base of black. If you want to make them sunnier and lighter mix them with off-white or cream. For emphasis, you can always mix in gold or silver metallics.

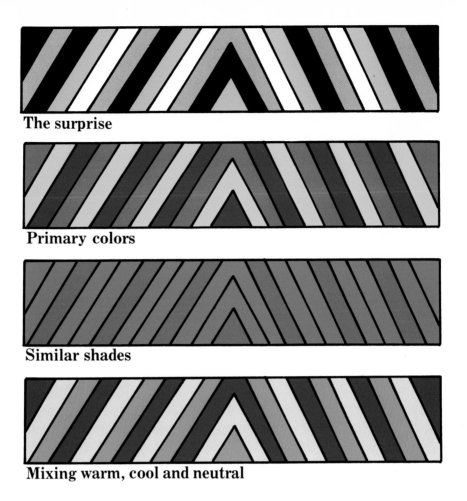

The surprise

Primary colors

Similar shades

Mixing warm, cool and neutral

Mixing warm, cool and neutral colors. At school we learned that red, yellow and orange were warm colors and blues and greens were cool colors and greys and beiges neutral. One of the more interesting ways to use color is to mix them completely, putting reds and greys together or beige and blue, or orange and blue. Use your imagination.

Color combinations. The great Bauhaus artist Joseph Albers spent his life studying the relationships between colors. He painted frames of color and proved that yellow had one quality when it was placed next to green and took on a completely different quality if placed next to red.

The following is a list of some possible color combinations each of which gives a different effect when placed next to another. Jot down next to each color combination what you feel when you look at them. Are they soft? Romantic? Innocent? Disturbing? I could tell you my opinion, but yours might be different, and you should start to develop your own conscious feeling and reaction to color. We all have such a unique color sense it is like our fingerprints.

Bright Red

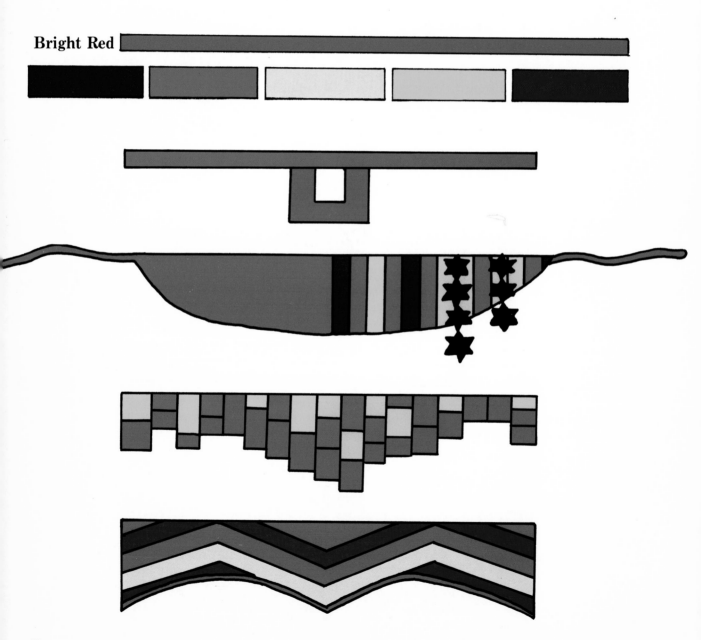

B

Royal Blue

C

Purple

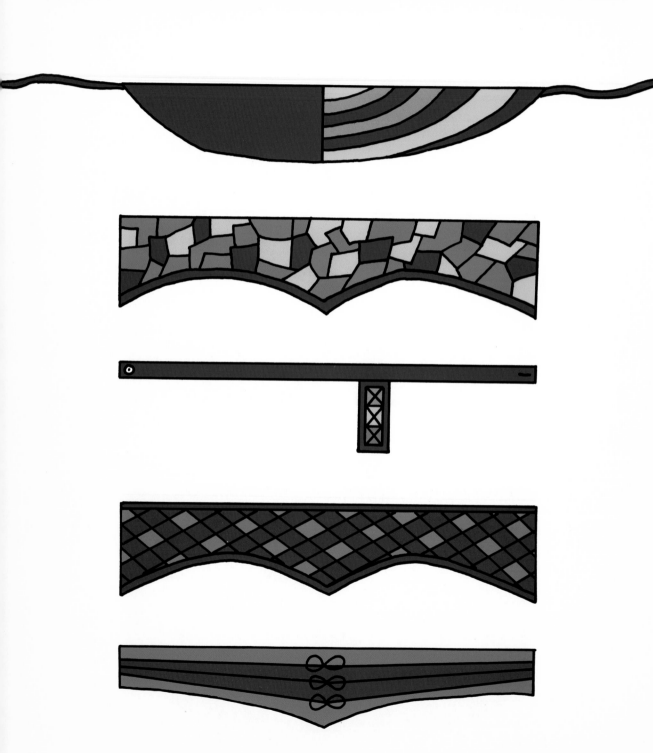

D

Green
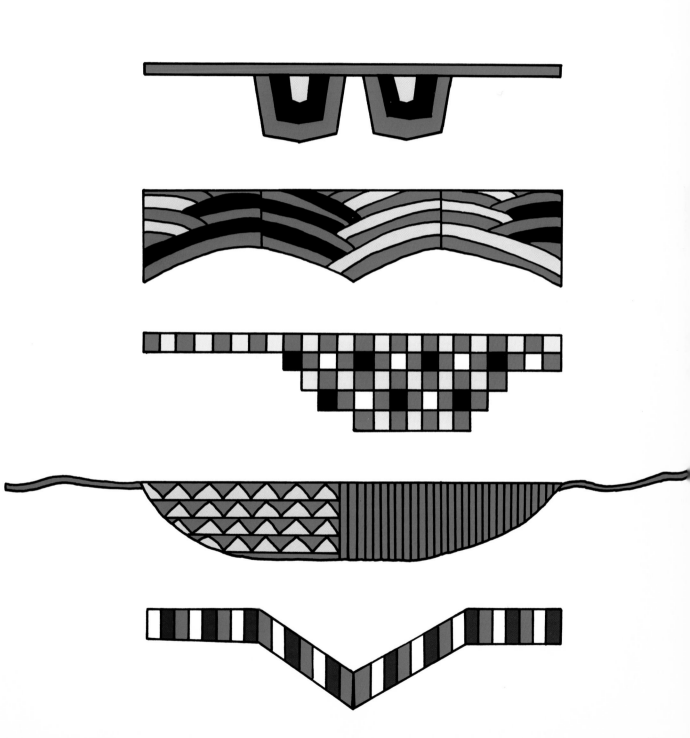
E

Burgundy

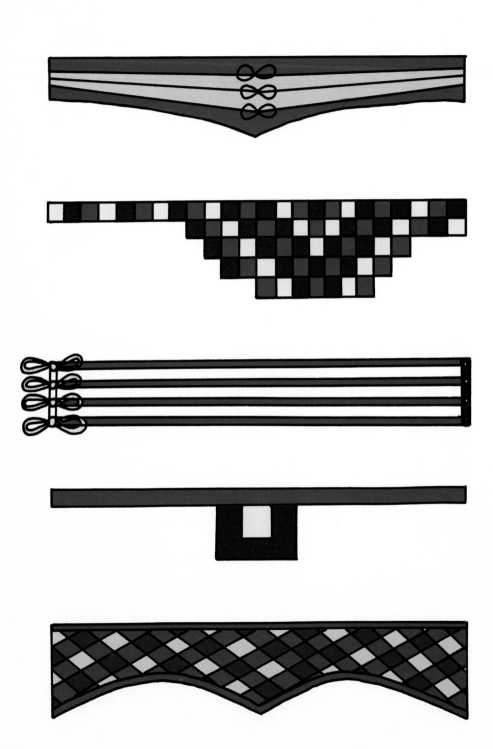

F

Turquoise

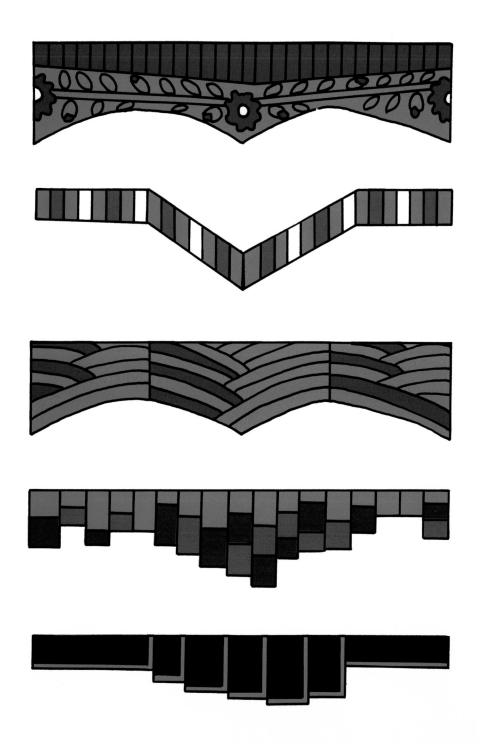

Beige

H

Nature as inspiration. They say God is the greatest artist. If we look around at things in nature, it would be hard to argue against this. We can't go wrong if we copy some of these combinations. Study the feathers of nearly any of the bird species. Look at the coloration on animals, the colors of flowers, or falling leaves in the autumn. Note the colors of mountains, or the sky at different times of the day. Butterflies, stones, wood, rainbows, metals and gems all could give ideas for beautiful color combinations. In summary, don't be afraid to experiment with color. And don't be upset if you are the only one who likes the combination. Color sense is unique, and there is no right or wrong.

Patchwork

Finishing individual patchwork. The systems for finishing the individual pieces are the same as those for finishing the whole belt. You have two different ways. These ways would be the same whether or not you decided to quilt the pieces.

1) You lay the top part over the bottom or the lining and stitch around the outside. Then you attach a binding tape to the bottom side, sew around and then pin on the top side laying over the seam. This is not the best way for these small pieces because it is difficult to do this on such a small piece.

2) You lay the front piece face to face with the lining and sew all around the outside leaving a small opening. You reverse the pieces through the hole and then close by hand-stitching. You could either topstitch with the machine or quilt by hand.

If you are using quilting with either of these two systems, the only difference would be that you include a layer of polyester or acrylic filling. Quilting would be important in these techniques because it adds body and texture. These small pieces must be firm and ready to stay in place and quilting would make that easier. See Illus. 18 and 19 for amplification.

Illus. 10. How to put the patchwork together.

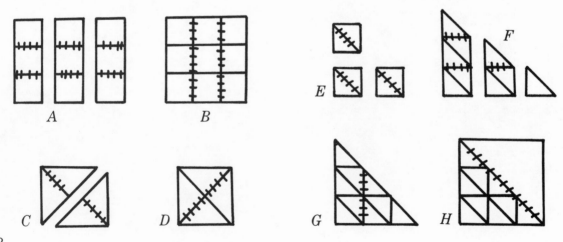

Illus. 11. How to make one section of the individual patchwork.

A. *Sew the two triangles together. Six go into one piece.*

E. *Hand-sew the closure.*

B. *Finished piece should look like this.*

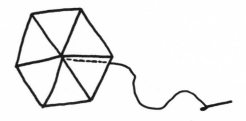

F. *Using a heavy thread, quilt the three layers to establish firmness.*

C. *Sew patchwork, wrong side up, to backing and stuffing, leaving a small opening.*

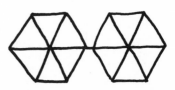

G. *Attach the individually finished pieces to a rope.*

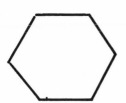

D. *Top section is left open.*

Finishing the Belt

There are two ways of finishing the belt. These methods are basically the same if it is to be quilted or not.

Finishing the Belt—By Machine

1) You lay the top part over the bottom part, the backing or the lining, and machine-stitch all around the outside (Illus. 12). You then use a binding tape, either bought or made (Illus. 13), attach the tape on the back, then bring it around to the front (Illus. 14), pin into place with the seam, then topstitch.

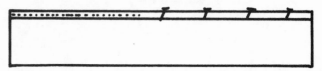

Illus. 14.

This method has the advantage of utilizing the tape as an additional part of the design and providing a new clean-looking finish. (See Illus. 15-17 for examples of topstitching.)

Examples of Topstitching

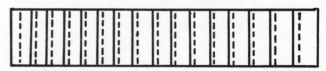

Illus. 15.

Illus. 12.

Illus. 16.

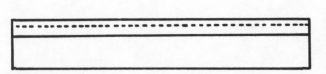

Illus. 13.

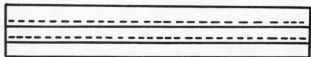

Illus. 17.

2) The second way is to lay the front side of the backing together with the front side of the front piece and stitch all around three sides, leaving a small opening at one end (Illus. 18). Turn the belt inside out and press flat with hands. Close the hole using hand-sewing. If desired, you could topstitch around the outside with a machine stitch. If not, you could quilt with a running stitch and achieve the same thing.

If you use quilting in either of these two techniques, the only difference would be that you include a layer of either polyester or acrylic fibre. Quilting adds texture and a fullness without making it heavier. If you use a light layer, it does not add to the weight. See appendix for examples of quilting stitches.

Embellishments. Belts can be embellished with special buttons or buckles, with sequins or beads or objects you have found. It's better if you find something that fits into a design, but you can build your design around an object. Try making a collection of odds and ends you might someday use even when you don't know exactly how. The opportunity will come up.

Closures. The closure is important. Without it, the belt has no function. The closure can be part of the design or it can be hidden. There are many different methods of closure. Belt buckles are perhaps the most common. Pin and loops, buttons, a simple tie, clasps, snaps and hooks and eyes are other possible methods (Illus. 20-27). If you think of something different, don't be afraid to use it.

Finishing the Belt—By Hand

Types of Closures

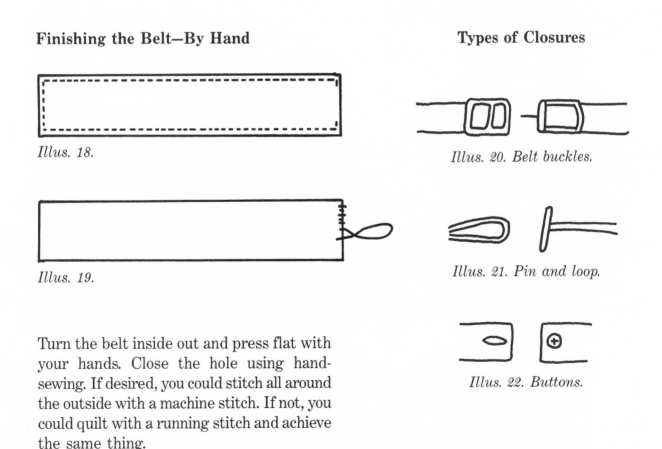

Illus. 18.

Illus. 20. Belt buckles.

Illus. 19.

Illus. 21. Pin and loop.

Turn the belt inside out and press flat with your hands. Close the hole using hand-sewing. If desired, you could stitch all around the outside with a machine stitch. If not, you could quilt with a running stitch and achieve the same thing.

Illus. 22. Buttons.

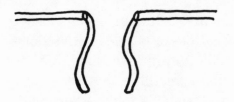

Illus. 23. Simple tie.

Illus. 25. Clasps.

Illus. 26. Snaps.

Illus. 24. Braided tie.

Illus. 27. Hooks and eyes.

BELTS

Illus. 28.
Quilted squares with crochet and cord ties.

Materials. Cottons, either solid colored or printed, silks or taffeta. Crochet border could be cotton yarn, white or colored, or metallic if a more elegant fabric is chosen. The filling should be acrylic or polyester fibre. Ties can be cotton cord or rope to match either the crochet fabric or the main material.

Color suggestions. Colors could be within one family, such as various shades of browns or blues. Golds and silvers are attractive for evening wear. Young children might enjoy primary colors; teenagers prefer shades of pink and purple.

Instructions. Decide how wide belt should be. Two to three inches would be a comfortable width with this design. Calculate how many blocks are needed to reach the desired length. Cut front pieces from one or several materials. Cut lining or back from desired material. Cut polyester or acrylic fill the same size.

With sewing machine, sew front block to back block right sides together, leaving a slight opening (Illus. 29). Place stuffing on top and then turn inside out. Close with invisible hand stitch. Iron three layers flat. If needed, topstitch with machine. Finish with a running stitch. Crochet border, using design of your choice (Illus. 30). Attach end ties to last square. Tie knot.

Illus. 29. Machine-stitch fronts and backs together, leaving opening.

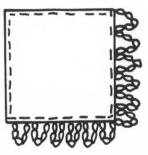

Illus. 30. Attach crochet into running stitch.

Alternatives. Design could also be done with leather or plastic. You might use transparent plastic and enclose a memento of some kind. You could try a heavy material and sew around and then fray the edges. Another possibility is using mirrors cut into small squares.

Illus. 31.
Quilted hexagons with crochet and cord tie.

See previous belt for materials, colors, instructions and alternatives.

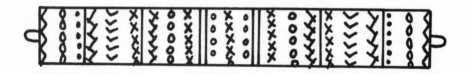

Illus. 32.
Embroidered belt.

Materials. A wide selection is possible. Wools, flannels, denim, cottons, silks, velvets or satins. Embroidery thread should be chosen to accent and complement the background material. Use acrylic or polyester lining and any type of backing desired.

Color suggestions. Any color works. I visualize beige wool with gold thread. Other possibilities are white with spring pastels or red with primary colors.

Instructions. Cut piece of material the desired size. Allow about an inch for shrink-age in the embroidery process. Select embroidery patterns and finish that stage. Sew it to backing and then line with fibre, closing it by hand.

Alternatives. Consider painting on material. Belt could also be sewn from large squares and then embroidered on top. Squares could be different hues of the same color family or totally different materials.

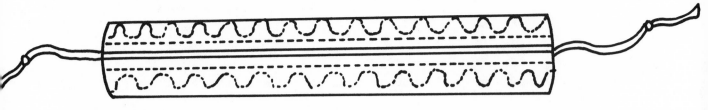

Illus. 33.
Quilted embroidered belt.

Materials. Any material—wools, flannels, silks, cottons—thread could be contrasting or the same color. Use acrylic or polyester fill and some type of backing.

Color suggestions. Blue or green with gold thread.

Instructions. Cut material to desired size, embroider pattern where desired. Sew it to back and lay filling on top. Reverse and close by hand-sewing. Topstitching can be done if desired. Attach tie across the middle of the belt and knot at desired length.

Alternatives. Consider appliqué or cutting out patterns of crochet or lace and sewing them on the front. Embroidery thread could be one-color or multi-color.

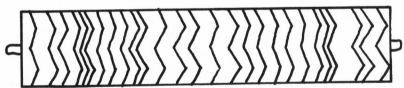

Illus. 34.
Embroidered quilted belt.

Materials. Lightweight fabrics either plain or printed.

Color suggestions. Greys with colored or gold thread would be nice.

Instructions. Cut material the size you want and mark pattern. Embroider it. If you are quilting, attach front to fill and quilt the two together. Finish it by either sewing the layers together back-to-back or by finishing the three layers and then sewing on a binding. Attach closures.

Alternatives. Make design, using patching or appliqué. Colors could be very close together in hue, such as all shades of purple or contrasting like black and white. You might try making them look like animal skins. Design could also be done by using smocking.

Illus. 35.
Embroidered quilted belt, using a child's drawing.

Materials. Cotton, wool, flannel, denim or any other heavy material.

Color suggestions. The background in white textured cotton with the figures embroidered in red and a small red binding around the outside.

Instructions. Decide how long and how wide the belt should be. Copy child's drawing onto the material and embroider it using either hand-stitching or machine-embroidery techniques. Finish it and quilt it in one of the methods described in the appendix and attach closures.

Alternatives. The pattern could also be either painted on or done in appliqué. You could follow the child during his developmental years and have him or her do a different drawing each year. The child would develop a sense of pride and you would have a wonderful reminder of those years. The belt could be made for child, parent or a proud grand-mother.

Road Race, *by 9-year-old Alexa Schaefer.*

Illus. 36.
Embroidered quilted belt,
based on child's drawing.

Materials. Cotton, wool, flannel, denim or any other heavy material.

Color suggestions. A light blue textured cotton background with the ducks embroidered in white with yellow and orange touches.

Instructions. Decide how long and how wide the belt should be. Copy child's drawing onto the material and embroider it, using either hand-stitching or machine-embroidery techniques. Finish it and quilt it in one of the methods described in the section on finishing and attach closures.

Alternatives. Instead of embroidery, the drawing could be either painted on or be done in appliqué.

The Duck Family, *by 9-year-old Alexa Schaefer.*

Illus. 37.
Quilted or embroidered belt.

Materials. Wools, satins, silks, cottons, whatever appeals to you. Thread could be matching or contrasting wools, cottons, or metallics.

Color suggestions. I prefer rich warm tones for this belt, but other colors are possible. Base your decision on what you might want to wear it with.

Instructions. Cut band to desired size. Mark pattern with light marking instrument. If it's embroidered, finish that part of the work. If it's to be quilted, place front layer and lin-

ing together and quilt the top two layers. When finished, attach back. It can be attached directly back-to-back and then reversed, or all three layers can be sewn together and a binding sewn on. Attach closing loops and buttons.

Alternatives. Design could be done in appliqué, patchwork or by attaching ribbons to make the design. Running stitch could also be done as a chain stitch or another embroidery stitch.

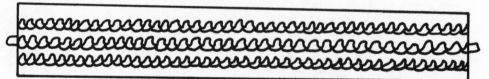

Illus. 38.
Smocked, embroidered or quilted belt.

Materials. Wool, flannel, cotton or corduroy. Embroidery could be done in cottons, silks or metallics.

Color suggestions. I see it in a dark turquoise with gold thread.

Instructions. If using smocking, cut the material long enough to include needed gathers for smocking. Finish smocking work and iron the folds all to one side. Attach lin-

30

ing and attach to backing. Put thin seam tape around the outside. Attach closures.

Alternatives. Embroidery or quilted. You could also attach a small piece of material to give texture where the circle is drawn.

You could attach buttons all across the row, or, for small children, perhaps use bottle tops or small stones.

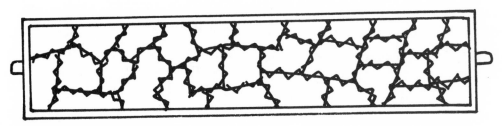

Illus. 39.
Crazy patchwork with embroidery and quilted.

Materials. I see it in silk with gold thread, but it could also be done in cottons with black thread or a mixture of more colorful ones. For small children a mix of primary colored cotton prints with bright cotton embroidery could be just the thing.

Color suggestions. Either subdued or bright, try grey wool with black thread.

Instructions. Cut band to required size. Take patches to be used and hem with a running stitch. Pin one into place in the middle of the belt. Add another one close enough so that the seam is covered. Continue until the whole piece is covered. Start herringbone stitch or any other embroidery stitch on top of the patches. Continue until finished. Add filling and backing and sew around the outside with a machine stitch. Add binding and then closure.

Alternatives. Embroider on background material without using different patchwork material. You could take magazine cuttings and a soft-tipped pen and make a fun throwaway belt for children.

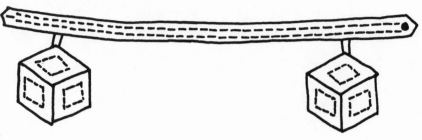

Illus. 40.
Patchwork pocket belt.

Materials. Cottons or another heavy material.

Color suggestions. Shades of browns and beiges.

Instructions. Decide how long and how wide the belt should be and design the pattern for the diamond pockets. Sew the pocket fronts together and quilt to the filling. Attach it to back piece on five sides, leaving the top of one side open. Sew two sections of lining together, while sewing in connecting tab.

Sew together with machine, leaving small opening to reverse and finish sewing by hand. Sew belt and attach closures. Attach pockets.

Alternatives. Paint on pattern. Quilt or embroider pattern on same material. Use primary colors and appliqué or embroider a letter or a number so that they look like children's building blocks. Use leather or plastic.

Illus. 41.
Quilted patchwork with embroidery.

Materials. I see this belt in solid-colored cotton squares with gold embroidery on top.

Color suggestions. Blues and greens with gold, primary colors with black, prints with colored embroidery thread.

Instructions. Decide width of belt and divide in half. Design a square measuring the width of the half. Cut out all necessary

squares and sew together. Sew on end pieces. Trace embroidery pattern on each square. Using a running stitch, embroider the pattern. Attach to back, reverse sides together, turn around, attach closures.

Alternatives. Design could be done in crochet, or formed using piping instead of the running stitch. A solid color could be used instead of patchwork squares.

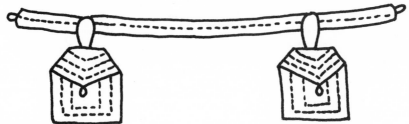

Illus. 42.
Quilted pocket belt.

Materials. Use cotton or another heavy material.

Color suggestions. Shades of brown and rose.

Instructions. Decide size of belt and pockets and cut pattern and material. Sew pocket to lining and backing and quilt. Sew together and put on binding and closure and top loop. Attach top loop to finished belt and attach closures.

Alternatives. You could experiment using unusual quilting threads, or embroider designs on the pockets. You could make the pockets out of different colors or of leather.

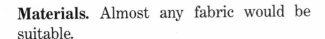

Illus. 43.
Strip belt.

Materials. Almost any fabric would be suitable.

Color suggestions. My preference would be shades of grey wool, but it could be done in sharply contrasting colors to give a gayer effect.

Instructions. Decide what width and length you want. This belt should ideally be rather wide. Divide it into five and make that the length of the strips. Cut five strips the same length and sew together for the middle section. Take total length and subtract the middle section, divide in two and make that the length of the side sections. Sew them together as illustrated.

Sew back to front and fill, in either of the ways described in the quilting section. Fix closures, whatever method suits you.

Alternatives. Pattern could be made with ribbons, could be one back material with embroidery on it, or one material with a quilting stitch on it.

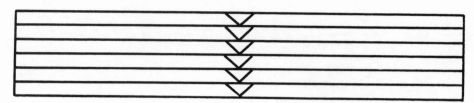

Illus. 44.
Strip patchwork belt.

Materials. Any material possible.

Color suggestions. My preference would be dark shades of violet with dark rose triangles, but any colors could be used, or the same color could be cut up so that the seaming makes the pattern.

Instructions. Decide on width. If you want the belt to be narrower, you could make less than five strips. Divide the width by the number of strips you want and design the triangle. Follow Illus. 45 so that the length of the triangle is twice the width. Cut ends of strips at the same angle as the triangle. Attach triangles at one side, iron, then attach triangles to the other strip. Sew all the strips together, making sure the triangles are lined up under each other. Finish in one of the ways described, either front to front, or all three layers finished together and binding attached. Attach closures.

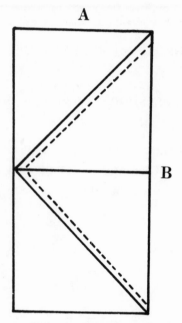

Illus. 45. Side A should be ½ Side B.

Alternatives. Pattern could be made, using the same material with embroidery or it could be made on the same material with a quilting stitch. Strips could be all the same color and the triangles could be in color. The triangles could be finished as separate pieces and attached to the front.

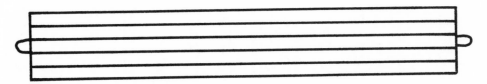

Illus. 46.
Strip belt.

Materials. My preference is for wools.

Color suggestions. Closely related colors such as shades of grey or warm tones, primary colors for children or lighter wear.

Instructions. Decide what length and width you want the belt to be. If you don't want it wide, use less bands. Divide width by the number of bands you want for the width of the individual band. Sew bands together and finish, either quilted or unquilted. Attach closures.

Alternatives. Pattern could be formed with quilting or embroidery stitch or by use of ribbons.

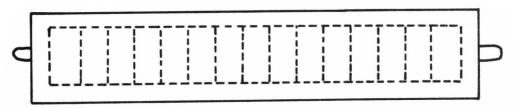

Illus. 47.
Quilted belt.

Materials. Silk, wool, cotton, whatever suits you.

Color suggestions. I see it in grey wool with gold thread, or raw silk with gold or silver thread, but, of course, any color could be used.

Instructions. Cut the background material to the size you want. Mark a quilting pattern, beginning with a frame around the outside and lines through the center, or any other imaginative pattern. Quilt the pattern, using a running stitch to front piece and the polyester behind. Finish and attach closures.

Alternatives. Middle strips could be done in different materials in patchwork pattern. Pattern could consist of embroidery stitches. Belt could be done in two separate pieces with the patches in front, forming one band and then attached to the back.

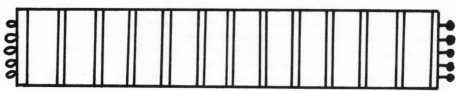

Illus. 48.
Folded tucked belt.

Materials. Satins, light wools or cottons.

Color suggestions. I see this in a light blue satin or raw silk.

Instructions. Decide what width and length you want. Make it longer depending on how many folds you want and how deep they will be.

Measure and mark folds so that they will be regular or where you want them. Stitch at the base of each until finished. Sew to backing, making sure folds are all in the same direction or the direction you wanted them. Attach closures.

Alternatives. Pattern could be made using embroidery, adding a ribbon or a strip of material, matching or contrasting. Strip of material could be the reverse side of the material used on the front.

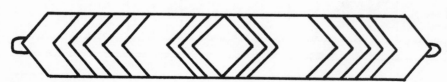

Illus. 49.
Patchwork strips.

Materials. Either cottons, satins, or silk. Because of the intricacy of the design, it would be easier to make in a lightweight material.

Color suggestions. Combinations of rose and dark green.

Instructions. Decide on width and length and what angle you want; then draw pattern. Sew belt in two halves, one half, with the pattern going in one direction and the other half, going in a different direction. Sew two halves together and finish up attaching closures.

Alternatives. Pattern could be made by sewing ribbons or other strips on the front. It also could be made with embroidery thread or quilting.

36

Illus. 50.
Patchwork strips.

Materials. Light cottons, either solid or printed, or silks and satins. A heavy material is difficult to work with because of the small pattern.

Color suggestions. Shades of burgundy and violet.

Instructions. Decide width, length and angle of the strip. Cut all pattern pieces and sew them together. If you have trouble with the angle, sew them all together and cut the angle afterwards. Sew to back and attach closure.

Alternatives. Pattern could be formed with either quilting stitch or embroidery stitch. You could use ribbons or any other type of strips.

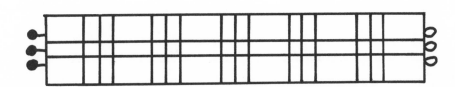

Illus. 51.
Patchwork plaid belt.

Materials. Any material will do.

Color suggestions. I see it in greys with a touch of red in the middle section. It might be interesting to try and mimic a plaid look.

Instructions. Decide the width and the length. Design the three cutting pieces: the small square, the larger square and the rectangle. That can be easily done by drawing them first on paper, measuring and then multiplying them until you reach the desired length.

Sew pieces together, using the technique described in the section on patchwork. Finish with backing and add closures.

Alternatives. Pattern could be formed, using quilting stitch or embroidery stitch. The same material could be taken and used so that the pattern comes from the seams.

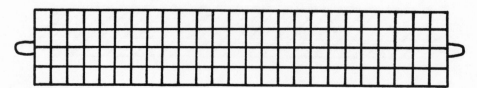

Illus. 52.
Patchwork belt.

Materials. Squares are easier to sew then some patchwork patterns; so just about any material could be used. However, it would be easier to use a light fabric.

Color suggestions. This pattern is interesting because colors make a big difference in the way it's used. (See the chapter on colors.) I prefer a mixture of many different black and white prints.

Instructions. Decide how wide you want the belt and how long. Next, what size square you want to use. About two inches square is a good size. It could also be bigger. Decide how you want to use the colors and the materials and draw it out first. Count how many squares you need of each color and cut them out. Lay them out on a table or a flat surface and arrange the colors as you want them. Sew them together row by row then strip by strip, making sure to get the seams matched well. Finish and attach closures.

Alternatives. You could use one material and have the seams make the design. Or you could make the pattern using either quilting or embroidery. Another possibility is the embroidering of a small flower or name of a friend on each of the squares.

Illus. 53.
Patchwork belt.

Materials. Although a lightweight fabric like cotton, satin or flannel is easier to work with, any type of material is acceptable.

Color suggestions. I see it in different shades of green but, of course, any colors are possible. You could change the pattern a lot, depending on your choice of colors and how you arrange them.

Instructions. Decide on width and length and how many bands you would like to have, then decide what width each band should be in order to give you the desired size. Make a cardboard cutting pattern and cut out all the pieces. Arrange on a table or flat surface, then sew them together row by row and attach all the rows. Finish either by quilting or just by backing the front piece. Attach closures.

Alternatives. Pattern could be formed with quilting or embroidery stitch, or by cutting out the same material and having the seams form the pattern. You could embroider something on each of the patches—perhaps friends' autographs or places visited. Pattern also could be formed with cut ribbons.

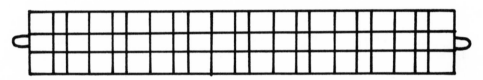

Illus. 54.
Patchwork belt.

Materials. Lightweight material would be easiest to work with.

Color suggestions. I visualize shades of dark turquoise with a small splash of red in the middle of the pattern.

Instructions. Decide how wide and how long the belt should be. Design the block, which consists of nine small squares (Illus. 55), then calculate how many pieces and how many blocks you need for the belt you are planning. Cut them all out and then sew row by row until you have a block; attach all the blocks together being very careful to match the seams. Finish in the way you have chosen and attach the closures.

Alternatives. Use a real plaid fabric and stuff and quilt it. Embroider or quilt-stitch

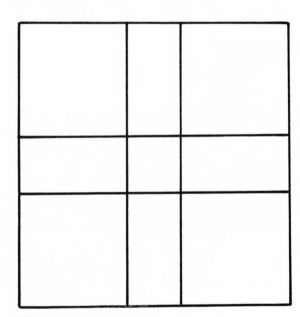

Illus. 55.

the pattern. Embroider a flower or some other small symbol in the middle of each square.

39

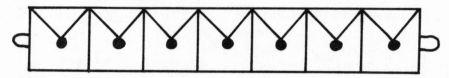

Illus. 56.
Patchwork-pocket belt.

Materials. Cotton prints or solids, denim or lightweight corduroy are recommended for children.

Color suggestions. Primary colors with black buttons.

Instructions. Decide how wide you want the belt to be and design a square with triangle closure. For each square cut a double square and a double triangle. Hem one of the squares on one side. Sew to the other square on three sides. Sew triangles together on two short sides and reverse. Sew triangles to square leaving an opening between the two squares. Attach button and loop. After all the pocket blocks are finished attach together in a long row. Attach backing and closures.

Alternatives. Do design in patchwork, without the pockets, using button for decoration. Vary the colors that are all the same or are differently colored. Design could also just be quilted in or embroidered.

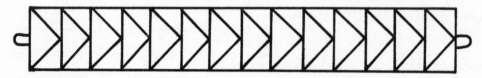

Illus. 57.
Patchwork belt.

Materials. Cottons would be easiest because of the small pattern of the belt. Lightweight wools or raw silk would also work.

Color suggestions. I see it in dark turquoise and purples.

Instructions. Decide how wide and how long the belt will be. Draft pattern on paper. Follow the drawing; the width of the block will be half of the length. Cut all the pieces and sew a small triangle on to one side of the larger triangle (Illus. 58). Iron and trim and then sew the other small triangle onto the other side of the large triangle. Iron and trim. Sew all the blocks together, finish in the described fashion, and attach closures.

Alternatives. Pattern could be formed by embroidery stitches, by quilting on the same material, or by using leather or plastics to make the belt.

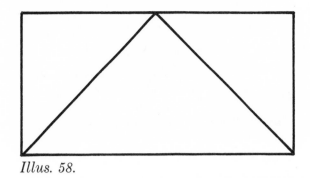

Illus. 58.

Illus. 59.
Patchwork belt.

Materials. Cottons are preferable.

Color suggestions. Greens and blues.

Instructions. Decide width and length. Each square will be the width measurement. Draft each block individually and make the pattern from the drawing. Cut the pieces, then assemble them one by one. Attach all the blocks and finish off either with a backing or quilted first, then backed. Attach closures.

Alternatives. Invent your own block designs. Embroider or crochet or quilt-stitch the pattern. You could use very similar colors so that the seam makes the pattern. Embroider or appliqué names of friends on the belt.

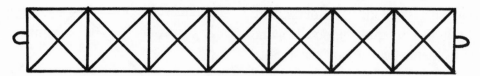

Illus. 60.
Patchwork belt.

Materials. Any material would be suitable—wools, satins or silks, cotton prints or plain material, leather or plastic. I have seen this design well done in corduroy where the pattern of the material makes an interesting texture as it is cut and faces different directions.

Color suggestions. I see it in gay primary colors.

Instructions. Calculate the width and length you want. The width should be the width of the square. Draw the pattern and cut. Sew the patches together. Sew the blocks together. Quilt or finish in the way you choose and add the closures.

Alternatives. Use one material and quilt the pattern. Use topstitching or folding technique to make the design. Embroider autographs or other motifs on the blocks.

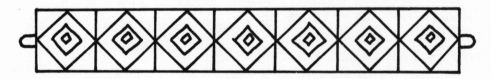

Illus. 61.
Patchwork belt.

Materials. Cottons or silk—any lightweight material. It would be difficult to sew this small a pattern with a heavyweight material.

Color suggestions. I see it in shades of purple and burgundy.

Instructions. Decide how wide and long you want the belt. Draw the block size to the desired width. Draw three squares, one on top of the other, in the middle. Make pattern and cut out material. Three blocks should be appliquéd one on top of the other. Attach all the blocks in a row. Finish and add closures.

Alternatives. Instead of using patches, you could paint, embroider or quilt the design.

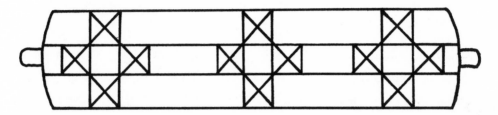

Illus. 62.
Patchwork belt.

Materials. Cotton or silk—a lightweight material. It is possible, but difficult, to use a heavy material because of the intricacy of the design.

Color suggestions. I see it in dark rose with black stars.

Instructions. Decide how wide and how long you want the belt and make the block the desired width. Cut pattern and stitch together (Illus. 63). Finish and add closures.

Alternatives. Quilt the pattern or embroider it instead of using patchwork. Try it in paper or leather.

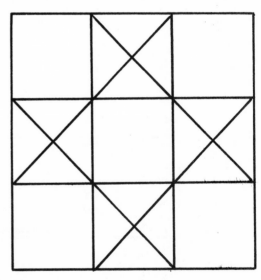

Illus. 63.

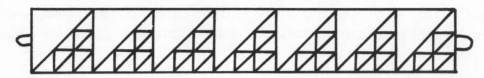

Illus. 64.
Patchwork belt.

Materials. Silk, satin or lightweight cotton—plain or printed. A heavier material would be difficult with such an intricate pattern.

Color suggestions. Shades of brown and beige.

Instructions. Decide on width and length and make the width the width of the block.

Make pattern for block and cut out. Sew together as described. Attach all the blocks together. Finish in the way described and attach closures.

Alternatives. Try leather or plastic. Pattern can be made using either quilting or embroidery on plain material.

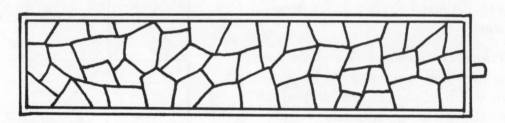

Illus. 65.
Appliquéd belt.

Materials. Any material will do, or you could mix materials. This is a crazy quilt pattern, but without the embroidery. You could easily mix velvets and silks and satins with cottons or whatever scraps you might have around.

Color suggestions. I see it in black velvet with strong shades of blue and purple.

Instructions. Cut a back piece to a specific size. It should about one inch longer than you want your finished belt to be. Take scraps of material and hem them. Tack them down with pins and then appliqué them into place so that no backing shows. Finish as desired and add closures.

Alternatives. Pattern could be quilted or embroidered on plain material. It could be done in leather or plastics. You could embroider autographs or any other symbols on the squares.

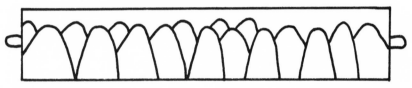

Illus. 66.
Appliquéd belt.

Materials. Cottons or other lightweight materials.

Color suggestions. I would either try it realistically with green mountains and blue sky or use a family of closely related colors, such as all shades of blue or green.

Instructions. Cut material for the sky in the width and length desired. Cut mountains the shape you want them and appliqué them onto the sky background. Finish and add closures.

Alternatives. Use leather or plastic. Outline mountains with gold or other embroidery thread.

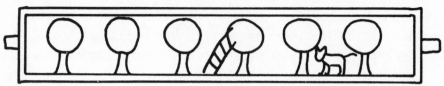

Illus. 67.
Appliquéd belt.

Materials. Lightweight cottons would be the easiest.

Color suggestions. Try making it realistic—trees either green or golden for autumn, blue or grey sky, brown dog and ladder.

Instructions. Cut a piece for the sky to the width and the length you want. Cut the pieces to be appliquéd and hem them. Pin them into place and then sew them with a blind stitch. It would also be possible to embroider the ladder and the dog and anything else very small. Finish and attach closures.

Alternatives. Paint the design or use leather. You could also embroider the pattern on the background.

Illus. 68.
Appliquéd belt.

Materials. Cottons or any lightweight material.

Color suggestions. I see it in realistic colors. White or cream background, pink flowers and green stems.

Instructions. Cut the background material to the size you want. Draw the pattern freehand on cardboard and cut it out. Trace on material desired and cut that out. Hemstitch flowers and stems and appliqué them onto background. Finish as desired and attach closures.

Alternatives. Use leather and either glue or topstitch onto background. Quilt design onto background using contrasting thread. Paint design onto material.

Illus. 69.
Appliquéd belt.

Materials. Any lightweight cotton or silk that can be worked with easily.

Color suggestions. Black background, green stem, different shades of red and pink flowers.

Instructions. Make pattern on cardboard. Trace it on material and cut out flowers and stems. Hemstitch each and appliqué it onto background. Finish and add closures.

Alternatives. Use leather and topstitch the design with machine. Work design with either gold thread or a chain stitch. Use same material but quilt in the design.

Illus. 70.
Appliquéd belt.

Materials. Cottons or any other lightweight material. Design is very small and would be difficult with heavy material.

Color suggestions. I like it in natural colors with a blue background, green stems and flowers in shades of red and pink.

Instructions. Cut background material the size of the finished belt. Make patterns freehand from cardboard and cut out from material. Hem all pieces and appliqué them against background. Finish and add closures.

Alternatives. Paint or stencil the design. Do design on plain material using gold thread. Use chain stitch or quilting stitch. Use leather and attach, topstitching with machine.

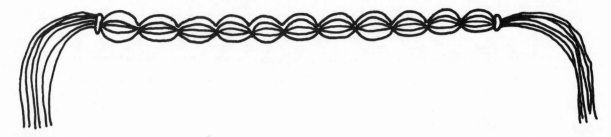

Illus. 71.
Fibre belt.

Materials. Strands of wool, cotton linen or whatever you like. You might even consider strips of material.

Color suggestions. I see it all in shades of blue and purple.

Instructions. Cut fibres slightly longer than desired for finished belt. Tie together tightly at intervals. Bind the ends and let fibres hang as far down in a fringe as you want.

Alternatives. Experiment with tying different kinds of materials together. You could even crochet different strips of material and put them together. You might try bands of lace or ribbons.

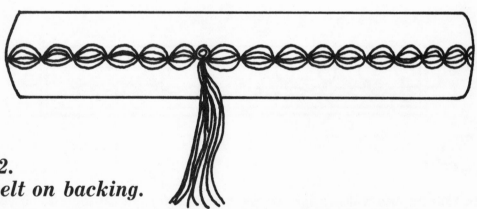

Illus. 72.
Fibre belt on backing.

Materials. Any type of fibres cut the same length. Backing could be cotton, wool, corduroy or any other middle to heavyweight material.

Color suggestions. Fibres could be mixtures of reds and browns. Backing could be a shade of beige or brown.

Instructions. Tie fibres together, using knots every few inches. Attach to backing. Quilt and finish as desired. Attach closures.

Alternatives. Embroider the design on top of the backing. Slit material and embroider so you can see through to backing. Use lace or crochet or other fibre for threads.

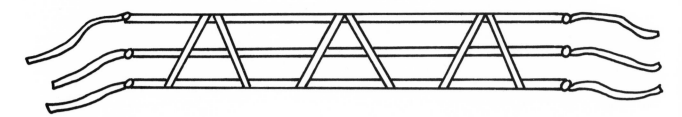

Illus. 73.
Fibre band belt.

Materials. Cottons or silk.

Color suggestions. My preference is silver blue.

Instructions. Decide how long and how wide you want the belt. Make the bands by sewing the strips together and then turning them inside out. If you want to make sure they don't roll, topstitch them. Knot three bands to the same length. Attach cross-bands to make it the appropriate width.

Alternatives. You could use ribbons, or you could sew leather or textiles to clear plastic. You could place the strips against a textile backing, and make the pattern by quilting or embroidery.

Illus. 74.
Fibre-tie belt.

Materials. Cottons, preferably solid colored.

Color suggestions. I see it in shades of burgundy and purple.

Instructions. Decide how long each of the bands should be. Sew strips into tubes and reverse. You can topstitch if you want. Sew one shorter strip for side piece going from the waist down however far you want. Attach strip to vertical band leaving enough to tie easily to the other side. Belt will be tied and untied in four places, each time it is taken on or off.

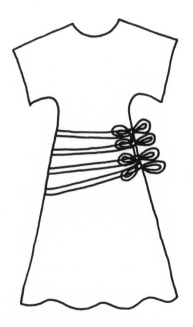

Alternatives. You could attach all four bands to one textile backing. The whole thing could be permanently tied and draped with a hidden closure.

Illus. 75.
Tie band girdle.

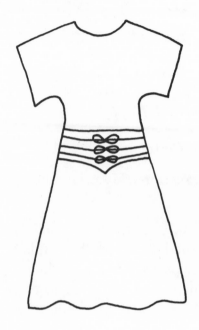

Materials. Silks or cottons—any fine material would do.

Color suggestions. Greenish turquoise. You could also use shades closely related to the backing.

Instructions. Cut and sew the girdle piece to the desired shape. This can be most easily done by measuring yourself and then trying a piece of material on until you get the shape you want. Take either cord or fibre or bands you make and tie them, and then sew the band down all around the belt. Closure could be either at the side or the back as you prefer. You could finish it with a backing, or it could be quilted and then backed.

Alternatives. Pattern could be embroidered or quilted on the front. Material in the backing could be changed in between each of the bands. You could use leather and then sew the cords on the front.

Illus. 76.
Banded belt.

Materials. Cottons, silks or any lightweight material. It would be difficult to work with a heavy material.

Color suggestions. I see it in reds with a different shade of pink in the middle of the flower.

50

Instructions. Decide on width and length. Cut and sew end pieces, leaving the ends open so you can slip in bands. Stuff and quilt them. Cut flower piece and put on front piece. Make the ten strips and sew seams. Reverse and attach to the middle of the side piece and the middle flower. Line flower by hand. Attach closures.

Alternatives. You could use ribbons in place of the bands. You could make the belt out of leather.

Illus. 77.
Banded quilted belt.

Materials. Cottons, wools or silks and satins. Just about any material would due for this pattern.

Color suggestions. I see the belt in light blue.

Instructions. Decide how long and how wide the belt should be. Cut end pieces, line and quilt them leaving the straight end open. Finish the three bands for the inside. Cut a diamond, stuff it, and attach the bands. Line the back of the diamond. Attach closures.

Alternatives. Use leather or plastic. Use ribbons or fibre in place of the bands. You could embroider or quilt the end pieces.

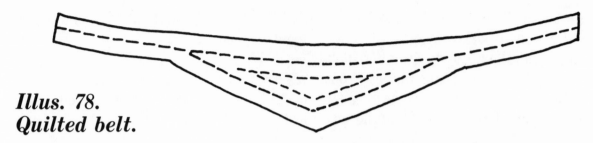

Illus. 78.
Quilted belt.

Materials. You could use any material for this belt from leather to cottons to silks or velvets, wools or flannel.

Color suggestions. I prefer it in red. Thread could be the same or an alternative color.

Instructions. Belt could be worn with point in the front or the back. Cut it to the shape you want. Put in stuffing and attach backing and quilt it in the desired pattern. Finish it and attach closures.

Alternatives. Pattern could be done in appliqué using different colors. You could attach fibres to the front instead of quilting.

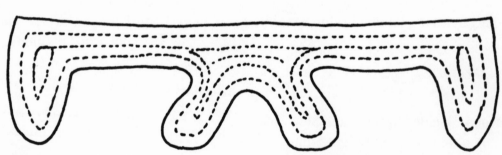

Illus. 79.
Quilted belt.

Materials. Any material which appeals to you, including leather or plastic.

Color suggestions. I visualize off-white or cream. The stitching could be in a contrasting color or several colors.

Instructions. Cut the belt, the backing and the filler to the size and shape you want. You could take your measurements, but the easiest way is to place material around your waist and hips and see how you want it. Quilt it in any pattern and finish it whichever method you prefer. Attach closures.

Alternatives. You could appliqué pattern on the belt rather than quilt it. Use leather and just topstitch or stitch contrasting leather colors on top.

52

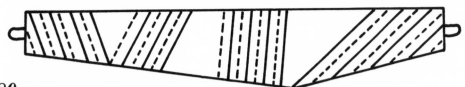

Illus. 80.
Topstitched folded belt.

Materials. Almost any material would do.

Color suggestions. I'd like a cream or off-white. Thread could be in the same color or a contrasting color—even a metallic.

Instructions. Cut the belt longer than the length you will want. Calculate how deep the folds will be and make it that much longer. First make the folds and then use either a running hand-stitch or a quilting stitch alongside. Sew it to filling and backing in the method you have decided on. Attach closures.

Alternatives. Use different embroidery stitches or only embroidery and no folding. You could put colored strips in place of the folded areas. You could use leather or plastic. You could attach ribbons along the folds.

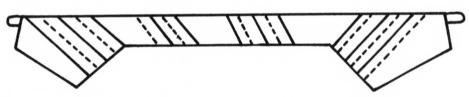

Illus. 81.
Folded and topstitched belt.

Materials. Any material you wish.

Color suggestions. I see it in beige with brown stitching.

Instructions. Decide how wide and how long you want the belt to be and cut a pattern. Try it on and see how the shape falls. Remember to leave some extra material for the folds. Topstitch either by hand or by machine. Finish in the technique you have chosen and add closures.

Alternatives. Patterns could be made by using ribbons or lace. It could also be made by using different materials in the form of stripes.

Illus. 82.
Appliquéd cut-out belt.

Materials. Use cotton, silk or any easily worked material. Avoid using a bulky material.

Color suggestions. I would use various shades of roses and pinks. For a small child it could be done in primary colors and made to look like a butterfly.

Instructions. Cut band to the desired length, hem and roll. It could be topstitched if so desired. Knot it a few inches from the end. Cut large shape for center piece. Cut backing and padding the same size, if you want it quilted and stuffed. Cut other pieces for the front of the motif. They should be hemmed and then appliquéd, using a blind hemstitch. Sew it to the backing and reverse it. Sew it to the belt.

Alternatives. The design could be simply embroidered. It could be done in leather or painted on.

Illus. 83.
Patchwork sculptured belt.

Materials. Just about any material would work on this one.

Color suggestions. I see it in shades of purples and burgundy.

Instructions. Decide on belt size. Draw the pattern, using shapes in any way you want. Cut out the pieces and sew them together, using the techniques described. Attach it to the main part of the belt. Cut lining to be the same shape. Sew the two layers together back to back. Attach closures. Belt could either close the middle (see Illus. 83) or there could be a hidden closure in the back.

Alternatives. You could use leather or plastic. Design could be painted on.

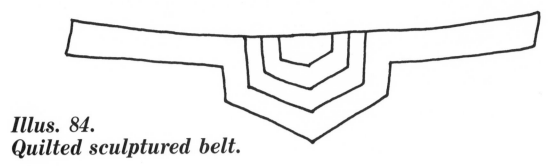

Illus. 84.
Quilted sculptured belt.

Materials. Just about any type of material.

Color suggestions. My preference is for shades of grey.

Instructions. Decide the exact shape and size and cut the pattern. It would be best to try it out first to see that it fits right. Cut material and draw quilting stitch. Quilt and then finish. Attach closures.

Alternatives. Design could be painted on. It could be made from leather or plastic. Each of the rings could be a different color and the thread could be one contrasting color or several.

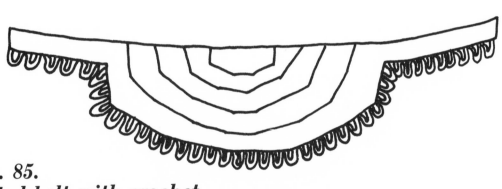

Illus. 85.
Quilted belt with crochet fringe.

Materials. Lightweight cotton, silk, velvet or wool.

Color suggestions. I see it in a greenish turquoise with a matching fringe.

Instructions. Decide the shape and size and cut the front, back and filling the same size. Choose the method of quilting and either draw the quilting pattern first and then finish, or finish first and then quilt it. Draw a running stitch all around the border of the belt and crochet a chain stitch border into the stitch. Attach closures.

Alternatives. Pattern could be done in concentric circles. A different material could be used for each ring. Instead of crochet, you could attach a ruffle or a fringe. Belt could be done in leather or plastic.

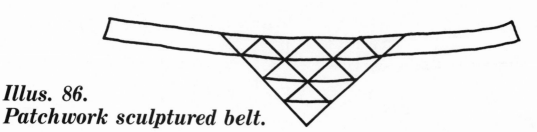

Illus. 86.
Patchwork sculptured belt.

Materials. Lightweight cottons, flannel or silk.

Color suggestions. I see it in shades of reds and purple.

Instructions. Decide how wide and long you want the belt. Decide how large the triangle will be. Three inches would be a good length. It could be larger or smaller or you could have more triangles there. Cut pattern pieces and sew together, using the technique described in the beginning. Attach side pieces and quilt. Attach backing and closures.

Alternatives. Use leather. Use just one piece of material and embroider or quilt the pattern on. Make the pattern in paper or plastics. Make the triangles in flaps and add a three-dimensional aspect.

Illus. 87.
Patchwork sculptured star.

Materials. Cottons, silks or any lightweight fabric.

Color suggestions. I see it in shades of blue and green closely matched up. It could be done in many colors or just in one and the same color so that the pattern would be formed by the seams.

Instructions. Decide how wide and how long you want the belt. Make the pattern for the star. Cut and sew the strips of each point

56

together. Then sew the star together. Attach the star to the lining and the backing and quilt. Attach to the belt and finish. Add the closures.

Alternatives. Make the pattern out of leather. Use either a quilting stitch or the embroidery stitch. Make it in primary colors for kids and metallics for evening wear.

Illus. 88.
Patchwork quilted sculptured belt.

Materials. Cotton, light wool, silk satin or other lightweight fabric. You could also use leather, plastic or paper.

Color suggestions. I see this in shades of brown, olive and beige, but the belt could be done in the same color with the pattern being formed through the quilting stitch.

Instructions. Decide the width and the length of the belt and cut the pattern. In order to sew you would have to divide the pattern into the part below the belt and the belt itself. When you have completed those individual sections, attach them. Finish the way you prefer, quilt first and then finish, or finish first and then quilt. Attach closures.

Alternatives. Take one piece of material and either quilt or embroider the pattern into it. Do the pattern in either primary colors or metallics for evenings. Pattern could be done by painting the pattern on. You could wear the design in the front or the back.

Illus. 89.
Appliquéd and quilted belt.

Materials. Cottons, leather or any stiff fabric.

Color suggestions. Shades of brown with an olive-colored belt.

Instructions. Decide the width and length of the belt. Design the pattern pieces and cut out the mateial. I would cut the material freehand to fit in where I wanted but it could be done with a pattern. Hem pattern pieces and appliqué into place. Sew the two side pieces, turn inside out and topstitch along the side if desired. Depending on the way you want to finish it, either quilt it first and then back it or sew it and then quilt it. Attach to side pieces and attach closures.

Alternatives. Use metallics or plain material and make the pattern with the quilting stitch. Embroider motifs on it.

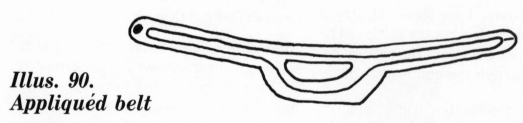

Illus. 90.
Appliquéd belt

Materials. Any type of material whether it be cottons, wools or silks.

Color suggestions. Shades of blue and grey.

Instructions. Decide how wide and how long you want the belt. Decide the shape you want the design and either cut a paper pattern and then the material, or cut the material directly freehand. Hem the pieces to be appliquéd and appliqué them to the background. Stuff and quilt and finish off the way you choose. Attach closures.

Alternatives. Use leather or primary colors. Use metallics for evening wear. Pattern could be made, using quilting stitch or embroidery stitch on a plain background.

Illus. 91.
Patchwork appliquéd quilted belt.

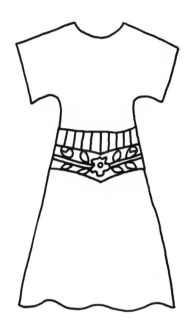

Materials. Cottons, silks or any lightweight fabric.

Color suggestions. I see it in blacks, purples and dark greens.

Instructions. Decide width and length of belt and cut patterns. Attach small strips to form a band. Attach bottom piece. Hem patterns to be appliquéd and appliqué them. Attach front piece to back and quilt, then attach closures.

Alternatives. Paint on the design. Use leather and topstitch, or do part or all of the design using either embroidery or quilting stitches.

Illus. 92.
Quilted girdle.

Materials. Heavy cotton or any material with body.

Color suggestions. I see it in dark green with black thread. Piping could be any coordinated color or the same. Burgundy would be attractive.

Instructions. Decide on the width and length of the belt and cut out a shape. Place it against the lining and the backing and draw the quilting pattern on the front. Quilt all three layers. Attach the piping as binding and attach closures.

Alternatives. Design could be made with patchwork using different colors or materials.

Another possibility is doing it in leather with machine topstitching.

Illus. 93.
Appliquéd belt.

Materials. Cotton, linen or any material which hangs well.

Color suggestions. My preference is for shades of green.

Instructions. Decide how wide and how long you want the belt. Decide size of the panel hanging down in front. Cut pattern pieces and appliqué the small square onto the larger one. Line front piece and sew to belt. Back the belt and quilt if desired. Attach closures.

Alternatives. You could add more squares and patterns. You could embroider on the front piece. You could line the front piece and turn it onto a pouch-like attachment.

Illus. 94.
Patchwork girdle.

Materials. Cottons, silks, satins or wools.

Color suggestions. Shades of blue.

Instructions. Decide how wide and how long the belt should be. Design the size of the square and cut the patterns out. Sew the squares together and then attach rows of squares to the next row. Line and quilt belt if desired and attach closures.

Alternatives. Design could be quilted on plain material or could be embroidered. Each square could be autographed and embroidered. Leather, plastic or paper could be used.

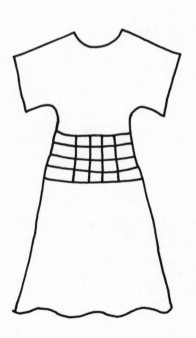

60

Illus. 95.
Patchwork belt with sash.

Materials. I prefer heavy cotton.

Color suggestions. Shades of purple and burgundy.

Instructions. Decide how long and how wide the belt should be. Decide the size of the sash and calculate how many of the patchwork patterns could be worked on the sash. Stuff, back and quilt the sash and attach to the belt. Line the belt and attach the closures.

Alternatives. Paint on the design. Embroider or quilt the design. Use leather or metallics. Attach embellishments to the belt.

Illus. 96.
Patchwork girdle.

Materials. Cottons, silks or other fairly heavy materials.

Color suggestions. Greys and blacks.

Instructions. Decide how long and how wide you want the belt. Try to form the pattern using material. Divide the belt into different rows of squares leaving one a little longer than the next. Work one row and then the next until they are all attached. Stuff and line belt and add closures.

Alternatives. Each block overlaps another adding texture. Pattern could be made by painting on different colors or embroidering or quilting the pattern. It could be embellished with buttons or other embroidery.

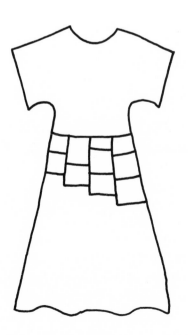

61

Illus. 97.
Patchwork tie-girdle belt.

Materials. Cottons or light flannel.

Color suggestions. Shades of green and blue.

Instructions. Decide width and length and cut pattern to try shape around your waist. Beginning in the middle of the back, one side will have squares and the other side will have stripes. It might be easier to make the two sides of the pattern and then cut the shape after that. Line and finish off, quilt if desired. Sew two ties and then attach them.

Alternatives. Pattern could be painted or embroidered on or quilted on a plain material using contrasting or similar thread.

Illus. 98.
Patchwork girdle.

Materials. Cottons or any other lightweight material.

Color suggestions. Shades of blues and purples.

Instructions. Decide width and length of belt. Make a sample pattern, either out of paper, or material, and drape the way you want it hung. Calculate how many strips of material you will need and then cut patterns. It might be easier to prepare a sheet of material of the strips and then cut the pattern from that. Line and attach closures.

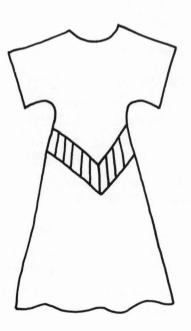

62

Alternatives. Paint on design. Use folding technique. Do design in either quilting or embroidery technique. Use leather and topstitch together.

Illus. 99.
Appliquéd belt with black topstitching.

Materials. Cottons or any other type of material desired.

Color suggestions. Shades of dark blue with black thread.

Instructions. Cut band the width, length and shape you want. Cut pattern pieces either from a pattern drawn before or just cut it out free hand. Glue with dry glue stick to the backing piece. Using a heavy black zigzag stitch, sew all the pieces down to the backing. Sew stuffing if desired and back and attach closures.

Alternatives. Design could be painted or quilt-stitched on, using metallic or other contrasting thread. It could be made from lightweight leather and topstitched.

Illus. 100.
Patchwork stripe girdle.

Materials. Any material desired.

Color suggestions. Shades of deep grey blue with a silver piping and binding.

Instructions. Decide the length and width and cut a pattern to try on and fit. Design the pattern out of cardboard or cut freehand. Sew one side together and then the other and attach the two sides. Place filler and backing and sew. Attach binding and closures.

Alternatives. Use appliqué technique and seam heavy black seams along the edges using the zigzag stitch. Pattern could be formed with either ribbons or lace or pattern could be painted on and then quilted or just quilted on plain material, using either the same color thread or heavy metallic thread.

Illus. 101.
Patchwork girdle.

Materials. Heavy cotton, silk or any other material.

Color suggestions. I see the color in cream or off-white.

Instructions. Determine how wide and how long you want the belt and draw the pattern. Cut patchwork and sew one half together and then the half going the other direction. Join at the middle. Line, back and quilt, then attach the closures.

Alternatives. Design could be painted on, it could be made with the quilting stitch or embroidered. It could be made, using ribbons or lace. It could be made of leather and then topstitched.

Illus. 102.
Patchwork girdle.

Materials. In this design you can mix different materials within the same belt.

Color suggestions. I see a mixture of golds and black velvet.

Instructions. Decide width and length and cut the backing to the size and shape desired. Hem all the patches to be applied. Lay one down in the middle and then apply the next on top of that making sure not to leave any gaps or openings. When finished, attach stuffing and backing and then add binding. Add closures.

Alternatives. Pattern could be made with either an embroidery stitch or a quilting stitch. It could be made of leather and then topstitched. You could embroider names or birds or flowers in each of the small patches.

Illus. 103.
Patchwork belt with sash.

Materials. Cotton or linen or heavy silk. Any type of material, which would hang well.

Color suggestions. I see the waistband in black and the strips on the sash in the colors of a rainbow—first yellow, then orange, then red, pink, purple, blue, etc. Or it could be primary colors for a younger child or in a mixture of metallics and elegant brocades for evening wear.

Instructions. Decide how wide and how long you want the waistband and the sash. Divide the sash into strips making sure it gradually gets wider towards the bottom. Sew the strips together and then line leaving it open at the top. Attach to the belt and line the belt. Attach closures.

Alternatives. Sash could be quilted or embroidered. Design could be painted on. You could embroider the sash with names or other objects.

Illus. 104.
Patchwork girdle.

Materials. Heavy cottons or silk.

Color suggestions. I see it in shades of blues and purples but it could be done in any color. It might be fun to play around with a checkerboard pattern or something that looks like a flag from car races.

Instructions. Decide how wide and how long the belt should be. Draw pattern and drape it around the waist to make sure it is what you want. Decide how large the squares should be and cut a pattern. Calculate how

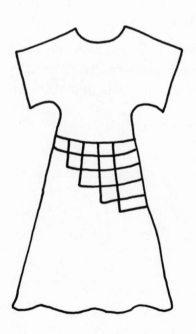

many squares you need of each color and cut them. Sew them together strip by strip, matching up the seam. Sew backing and attach closure. Quilt if desired.

Alternatives. Pattern could be quilted in or embroidered on plain material. Pattern could be painted on or worked in either leather or plastic. You could embroider either a small flower or a name or some design in the middle of each square.

Illus. 105.
Patchwork girdle.

Materials. Any material.

Color suggestions. I see it in different shades of purple and turquoise with a burgundy piping border.

Instructions. Decide how wide and how long and drape material around your waist to make sure it will hang right. Cut pattern and blocks. Sew a thin border around the first block on three sides. Sew borders around other blocks on two sides and attach. When finished, add stuffing and backing. Quilt if desired and add closures.

Alternatives. It could be done using machine appliqué techniques. You could also embroider either specific designs or an overall pattern on the blocks.

Illus. 106.
Patchwork hip-hugger belt.

Materials. Heavy cottons or any other heavy-weight material needed to give body to the side pieces.

Color suggestions. I would make this in shades of red and grey.

Instructions. Decide how wide and how long you want the belt and design the shapes of the side pieces. Try it with samples of material and see how it falls. Draw pattern and cut material. It should be done in bars and sewn one on the other. After that, match up seams. Back or quilt as desired leaving upper end open. Sew into belt. Line belt and attach closures.

Alternatives. Another way to complete the same design would be to do it in appliqué. It could either be done by hand or machine. By hand, you should hem the patches and appliqué each to the next one. By machine, dry stick-glue it to the piece underneath and then zigzag using heavy black thread. Design could also be painted on or embroidered or quilted with a running stitch into plain material. It could also be finished as pockets. Leave opening and hem where desired.

Illus. 107.
Patchwork girdle belt.

Materials. Cottons or other heavy materials.

Color suggestions. Different shades of green and blue, or it could be done in one color and the seams and the cutting line make the pattern.

Instructions. Decide how long and how wide the pattern should be. Make a pattern and try it out on your waist. Cut the strips, remembering that each should be slightly wider at the bottom depending, of course, on your measurements, and each should be a little longer than the previous one.

When finished, cut the filler, if desired, and the lining to be the same size and shape. Machine-stitch the backing to the front and turn. Iron and stitch if necessary. Attach closures.

Alternatives. Design could be painted on. It could be embroidered, or the pattern could be made using the quilting stitch. It could be made out of leather and topstitched or it could be done in a machine appliqué technique where you zigzag with a heavy black sewing-machine stitch.

Illus. 108.
Wraparound girdle.

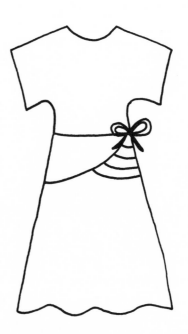

Materials. Heavyweight cotton or other material.

Color suggestions. Turquoise and beiges or possibly black with rainbow-colored stripes.

Instructions. Decide width and length of belt. Cut into the shape you want and drape it around your waist to see that it falls correctly. Stripes could be done with patchwork techniques, machine appliqué with black zigzag along the edges or hand appliqué. Attach striped section to plain section. Attach to backing already cut to the same size. It could be quilted if desired or merely machine-stitched back to back. Sew ties and add to corners.

Alternatives. Pattern could be either painted on or done in batik. It could be made of leather or a mixture of leather and other materials.

Illus. 109.
Patchwork wraparound girdle.

Materials. Lightweight cottons or any other lightweight material.

Color suggestions. The triangles in dark cherry red, alternating with turquoise and purple. The stripes could be the same color scheme.

Instructions. Decide how wide and how long the belt should be. Cut a pattern and try it around your waist to make sure it hangs as you want. Make the triangle pattern. It is usually easiest to make the width twice the height. It is also easier to make a straight piece of material about the same size of the finished belt and treat it as material off the bolt. Take the belt pattern and cut out the belt. The stripes can end at the hip or they can continue around to the middle of the back.

Add batting, if desired, and cut lining the same size. Sew it together back to back and then reverse. Make closing ties and attach them.

Alternatives. Paint on the design, or use metallics. Make the design, using either embroidery or a running quilting stitch. Use leather or plastic. You could finish the triangles as separate pieces and attach them to the main piece at the corners.

70

Illus. 110.
Sculpted 3-D wraparound girdle.

Materials. Cotton would be the best.

Color suggestions. Make the girdle part in a pale lime green and the flowers in white with yellow centers.

Instructions. Decide width and length of belt and make pattern. Try out the pattern around your waist to be sure it hangs well. Cut the top material and the back. If it is to be filled then cut both the same size and sew back to back and reverse. Quilt or topstitch as desired. Finish flowers individually and sew to girdle section. Add closures.

Alternatives. Pattern could be done in leather or plastic. Some of the patterns could be embroidered or topstitched onto the background.

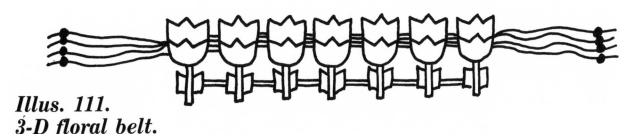

Illus. 111.
3-D floral belt.

Materials. Cottons.

Color suggestions. Try the flowers in real colors—with green stems, pink flowers and white ties.

Instructions. Make pattern for the size you want. Patch design together, then stuff and quilt it. Connect the flowers with the tie cords. Place either a bead or a tie at the end.

Alternatives. Pattern could be painted on or appliquéd instead of patched.

Illus. 112.
3-D belt.

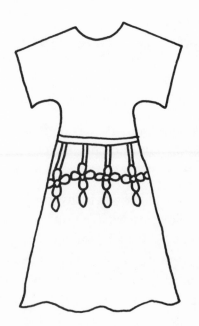

Materials. Cottons.

Color suggestions. Green stems and red flowers with yellow centers.

Instructions. Decide width and length of belt. Decide how wide you want the flowers to be; make the pattern and finish individually. Attach to each other and to the belt. Attach closure.

Alternatives. You could attach the flowers to the front of a girdle-like belt if you wanted more stability in the design. It could be made in leather or plastic. You could try to make different types of flowers: roses, irises, carnations, etc.

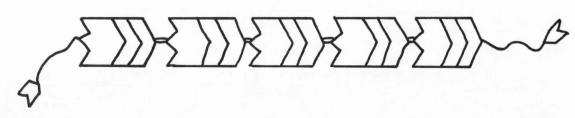

Illus. 113.
3-D appliquéd belt.

Materials. Cottons.

Color suggestions. I like it in realistic colors—shades of green and then pink. Ties could be white.

Instructions. Decide how long and how wide the belt should be. Design pattern so that it fits your dimensions. Cut pieces and sew together. Attach one flower to the next and attach end cord.

Alternatives. Design could be either painted on or quilted. It could be done in batik and topstitched. You could think of other floral patterns.

Illus. 114.
3-D belt.

Materials. Cottons.

Color suggestions. Different shades of red and pink with a yellow center and a green connecting cord.

Instructions. Decide how long you want the belt to be and how wide the flowers. Design a pattern for the petals and the inside center. Cut the pieces out, including the center and the backing. Sew pieces together around the edges and turn inside out as described earlier, finish by hand and attach to cord until finished. Knot cord a short distance from the end.

Alternatives. You could make the flowers from leather or plastic. You could attach the flowers to a quilted band background. You could try to make different types of flowers.

Illus. 115.
3-D floral belt.

Materials. Cottons would be best.

Color suggestions. I would make the leaves and the stems in olive green and the rose in pinks and yellows.

Instructions. Decide how long the belt should be and how large you want the rose to be. Design the pattern for the parts and cut backing for the large flower, the leaves and the bud. Sew the back to the front back sides together, add stuffing reverse and close by hand. Appliqué either by hand or machine the middle of the flower onto the backing and finish in the same way. Attach all the parts to the cord.

Alternatives. You could use alternative materials such as leather, plastic or silk. You could prepare a quilted background and attach the part to that. You could either paint the design on a background or do it in batik. You could embroider the design on a backing.

73

Illus. 116.
3-D patchwork belt.

Materials. Just about any type of material would do.

Color suggestions. I would do it in various shades of red and deep rose.

Instructions. Decide how long you want the belt and how large you want the hearts. Make a pattern for the heart and cut the front, the backing and the filler all the same size. Sew hearts in the method described earlier on finishing up individual pieces. Attach to cords. Put knots or beads at the end of the cords.

Alternatives. You could paint the design on a background and quilt the whole thing. You could embroider names or flowers on the hearts.

Illus. 117.
3-D belt.

Materials. Cottons.

Color suggestions. Make it in a lion's colors: golden brown with black eyes and red lips.

Instructions. Decide how long you want the belt and cut the strip to be seamed, reversed and topstitched. Decide how large and how tall you want the animal to be and make a pattern. Cut front, stuffing and back all at once and complete as described earlier in the section on finishing individual pieces. You might want the lion's mane to be a different color and you could appliqué that against the lion's head. Take DMC no. 5 embroidery floss or something else suitable and embroider eyes and mouth. Attach to cord.

Alternatives. Try to make other animals or birds of your own design. Animal could be painted, batiked or sewn onto a background piece. You could use leather or plastic.

74

Illus. 118.
3-D patchwork belt.

Materials. Cottons.

Color suggestions. I would make the cars in primary colors with black wheels.

Instructions. Decide how long and how wide you want the belt to be and design the car. It does not have to be realistic and could have as much personality as you want. Cut the top pieces in one color, and the backs with fillings all at the same time. Sew them together in the technique described earlier. Cut out the wheels from a different material and appliqué them on. You could either embroider the windows or appliqué a different material. Attach the cars to the three cords. Attach a bead or make a knot at the end of each cord.

Alternatives. You could either paint or batik the design on a background belt. You could try to make different types of cars or bikes or planes, maybe even boats. You could use leather or plastic.

Illus. 119.
Appliquéd quilted belt.

Materials. Almost any material that is easy to work with.

Color suggestions. I see it in white with black notes and lines. You could also use different colors for each of the bars.

Instructions. Decide how wide and how long you want the belt and cut the background piece. Add the black strips either by using embroidery, a machine zigzag or a thin black band. Cut the notes out and appliqué them onto the band. It might be easier to finish the circles separately, fill them and attach them to the belt. Add a band to each end and add closures after sewing on the backing and adding filling.

Alternatives. It could be painted on. It could be done with leather or metallics.

Illus. 120.
3-D patchwork belt.

Materials. Easiest would be a cotton material or felt.

Color suggestions. I see it in shades of brown and beige. I would make the eyes and the whiskers and tie cord in a darker brown or a black.

Instructions. Decide how long the belt should be and how large you want the cats. Design the cats. You could do a realistic drawing of a cat, or you could merely draw circles with points for ears. Cut the pattern pieces. Sew the three layers of the ears together leaving the base part open. Sew the

eyes on the face. Sew the face pieces together leaving the top open. Slip the ears into the top of the head and attach either by hand or machine. Attach whiskers to cat's face under nose. You could embroider or appliqué nose. Attach beads to the end of the tie cords.

Alternatives. You could paint the cats' faces on plain material. You could embroider them. You could appliqué them directly onto a quilted belt background. You could make it using other animals.

Illus. 121.
3-D patchwork belt.

Materials. Material could be a heavy cotton, felt or any other firm stiff material.

Color suggestions. I see the dogs in a honey-colored beige with white eyes and black noses.

Instructions. Decide how long and how wide you want the belt and then design the dog. You could make your own version or simply copy the easily drawn circle head pattern.

Cut out the pieces. Cut three layers for each animal, the front, the stuffing and the backing. Sew the ears together back to back and finish by hand. Sew the eyes on the face either with embroidery or appliqué techniques. Sew the nose with the machine, leaving the top part open to be attached to the face. Sew the three layers of the face, making sure to include the ears in the sewing. Leave a small opening to turn the face near the nose area. Lay the nose on the face and attach either by blind hemstitch or by machine. Attach beads to cord or knots and attach cord to dogs.

Alternatives. Faces could be done in leather or plastic. You could experiment with other types of animals or dogs. You could paint the face of the dog. You could either embroider or appliqué the dog into a quilted belt background or attach the faces to a belt.

Illus. 122.
3-D patchwork belt.

Materials. Cotton, felt, or any other stiff material.

Color suggestions. I would make the sheep in white with black faces and black legs.

Instructions. Decide how long and how wide you want the belt. Design the sheep and cut the pattern. Cut out the material. Sew the three layers of the legs together, leaving the tops open. Sew the face to the top hair, embroider the face and attach to backing and stuffing, reverse leaving the neck open. Sew the front layer of the body to the stuffing and the backing, including the legs in the machine-stitching. Leave the part around the head open, slip in the head and finish either with hand-stitching or machine-stitching. Attach to the cord or rope belt.

Alternatives. Paint the sheep on a quilted belt background. You could embroider or appliqué the sheep to a background or you could finish the sheep and attach them to a background to give the belt more stability.

Illus. 123.
3-D patchwork girdle.

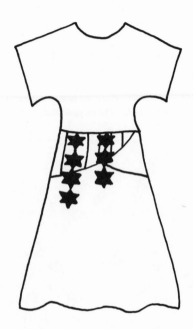

Materials. Cottons would be best.

Color suggestions. Red, white and blue would be effective.

Instructions. Decide how wide and how long you want the belt to be. Decide what the cut of the girdle should be; how it could be the most flattering. It is best to cut a piece of material and fit it around the waist to see how it falls. Make the pattern for the stars and cut the front, the stuffing and the lining. Sew the stars together as described in "Basics" section. Cut the stripes for the right half of the belt. They can either be sewn together or they can be attached one-by-one to the backing. Attach the stars to each other and then to the top of the girdle. Attach front to backing and stuff if desired. Attach closures.

Alternatives. Paint the pattern on a quilted girdle. Stars could be made out of metallics or aluminum foil. Belt could be made out of leather.

Illus. 124.
3-D patchwork.

Materials. Cotton, felt or other stiff material.

Color suggestions. Shades of gold and yellow.

Instructions. Decide how wide and how long you want the belt. Design the pattern for the stars and cut the front layer, the backing and the stuffing all the same size. With the front

78

of the front layer and the backing sew with the machine all around the outside, leaving just a small opening to turn it. Place the stuffing before turning it. Close the opening either by hand or machine and iron. Topstitch if necessary. Attach to cord or rope tie.

Alternatives. Stars could be painted on a background or finished star could be applied to textile belt background. You could make them in red and white stripes and attach to several blue cords, giving a more patriotic look.

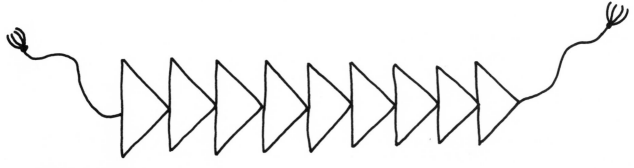

Illus. 125.
3-D patchwork belt.

Materials. Cottons or wool would be best. It should be made of something firm.

Color suggestions. Shades of purple and dark reds.

Instructions. Decide how long and how wide you want the belt to be. Design the individual triangles. The width should be twice the height. Make pattern and cut triangles, front, stuffing and back. Sew them together as described in the beginning. Attach them to each other in the middle and attach the cords. Knot, or leave a bead or a tassel at the end.

Alternatives. The triangles could be individually finished and then sewn onto a quilted belt. They could be painted on a background or appliquéd.

Illus. 126.
3-D patchwork belt.

Materials. Cotton or felt.

Color suggestions. My preference would be different shades of reds and oranges.

Instructions. Decide how wide and how long the belt should be. Design the individual hexagons and divide into six. Cut out the fronts with the stuffing and the backing and sew as described in the chapter on "Basics."

Attach each section to the other and attach the cords at the end. Knot a bead or tie a knot at the end.

Alternatives. Pattern could be made of leather or painted on a background belt. The sections could be finished individually and then attached to a quilted belt background.

Illus. 127.
3-D patchwork belt.

Materials. Cotton or felt.

Color suggestions. Shades of browns, beiges and olive green. It could be done in primary colors for childern.

Instructions. Decide how wide and how long you want the belt and make the pattern for the diamonds, which would make the individual block. Cut the front pieces with the stuffing and the backing. Sew the three diamonds to make the individual block and then sew as one block to the next. Sew the

back pieces together in the same way and lay the stuffing on top. Sew one band to the other, leaving a small opening. Reverse and close opening. Quilt between the blocks and along the seams if necessary to make them lie flat. Attach closures.

Alternatives. It might be interesting to appliqué or embroider letters and numbers on the blocks as if they were children's building blocks. Make them out of leather or paper. You could make smaller blocks on top of the blocks as they are.

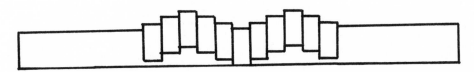

Illus. 128.
3-D patchwork belt.

Materials. Cottons or leather.

Color suggestions. It could be black with the small rectangles made out of rainbow colors or khaki with various shades of browns and beiges.

Instructions. Decide how wide and how long the belt should be. Finish up the base piece. It could be just lined or it could be lined and quilted. Decide the size of the rectangles and cut the front, middle and back. Sew around the outside and then turn inside out as described earlier. They could be stuffed or just lined if preferred. Attach them individually to the back piece and attach closures.

Alternatives. You could embroider on each of the rectangles. You could stuff each differently so the texture would be varied.

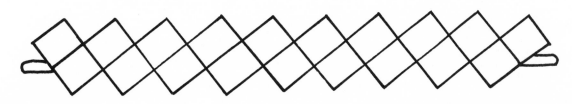

Illus. 129.
3-D patchwork belt.

Materials. Cottons or any heavy material.

Color suggestions. Blacks and violets.

Instructions. Decide how wide and how long the belt will be and then design the individual square. Cut the squares and sew them together row by row and then attach them. Lay that band across backing material and stuffing and cut it. Sew them together around the edges and then reverse. Close the opening and attach the closures.

Alternatives. Design could be all one material or it could be bars instead of squares. You could embroider on each of the squares.

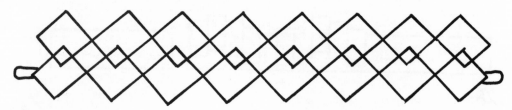

Illus. 130.
3-D patchwork belt.

Materials. Cotton, silk, satin or wool.

Color suggestions. I would make the small square in the middle red and do the outside in shades of grey and black.

Instructions. Decide how wide and how long you want to make the belt. Design the pattern pieces and cut and piece together. Place them over the stuffing and the backing and stitch together around the outside, leaving a small opening. Attach closures.

Alternatives. Make the belt out of leather or plastic. Embroider a design on it. Make long strips and weave the pattern instead of doing it in patchwork.

Illus. 131.
Patchwork sash.

Materials. Silk, satin, wool, or cottons.

Color suggestions. I see it in shades of blue and turquoise.

Instructions. Decide the shape and measurement of the sash. It might be easiest to drape a piece of material on your shoulder to use as a pattern. Design pattern piece and cut all desired patches; sew patches together. Cut backing and sew around borders with machine, leaving hole to turn it. Turn and then close the hole.

Alternatives. Embroider on the sash. Paint or batik design. Make it out of metallics or leather.

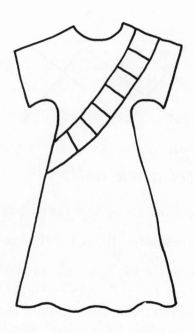

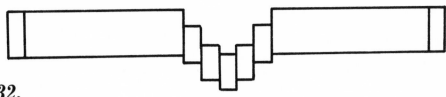

Illus. 132.
3-D patchwork belt.

Materials. Cottons or any stiff material.

Color suggestions. I would make the long side bands in white and the rectangles in colors of the same family. The end rectangles could repeat the colors from the middle.

Instructions. Decide how wide and how long the belt will be. Design the pattern for the small rectangles. Cut the pieces out. Sew the small rectangles together. Put them against the filling and backing and sew wrong side out, then reverse. Leave the sides of the end rectangles open. Sew the small rectangle to the end of the longer piece; sew the backing and the filling on the long end pieces, leaving the inside ends open. Attach the three pieces and sew either by hand or machine. Attach closures.

Alternatives. Embroider on the belt or the rectangles. Belt could be made of leather or plastic.

Illus. 133.
Patchwork strip sash.

Materials. Cottons, silk satins, or velvets.

Color suggestions. Shades of purples and blues or in metallics and matching silks and satins.

Instructions. Decide the exact shape and size of the sash and design the pattern. Cut the pieces and sew them together. Line and sew the belt and lining.

Alternatives. Design could be painted on or could be one material and quilted. It could be made of leather.

Illus. 134.
Double patchwork sash.

Materials. Cottons or metallics, heavy silks, satins—anything pliable but with body.

Color suggestions. Shades of purples and blues.

Instructions. Drape material over shoulders and make the pattern, being sure it falls the way you want. Design the pattern pieces and cut desired squares and the two stripes. Piece them together and attach the two sashes.

Alternatives. Design could be painted on. You could embroider on the squares. It could be made of leather or any unusual material.

Illus. 135.
Patchwork sash.

Materials. Cottons, silks or satins.

Color suggestions. Shades of red and oranges with a black belt.

Instructions. Drape pattern over your shoulders to make sure it is the length and size you want. Design the square patch pattern and cut out the material. Sew the two strips together and then attach to each other being careful of the seams. Attach backing. Sew band and back and attach to sash.

Alternatives. Embroider motifs on the patches. Interspace metallics in the design. Do design in batik or paint.

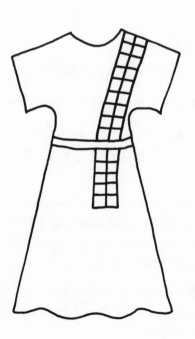

Illus. 136.
Appliquéd sash.

Materials. Cottons, silks, organdy or any other lightweight material.

Color suggestions. Pale pastels: light green stems and leaves, pale pink flowers on a white background.

Instructions. Make model for the size sash you want and try it to see that it falls right. Design patterns for leaves, rose and bud. Cut the patches and hem them. Appliqué them to a background. Line and reverse and attach to each other.

Alternatives. Paint the pattern on the sash. Do it in metallics or embroider on it. You could make it in bold primary colors for children. It could also be done in soft leather or suede.

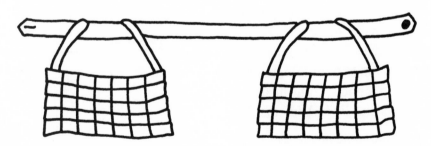

Illus. 137.
Patchwork pocket belt.

Materials. Cottons or other heavy materials would do.

Color suggestions. I see it in shades of green and blue.

Instructions. Decide on length and width of belt. Decide the size and shape of the pockets and make the square pattern. Cut out the pieces and sew the front sections together row by row. Cut the lining and backing for the pockets. Sew the three sides of the outer piece together and the three pieces of the inside pocket. Sew together on the top with a machine and leave a small hole to reverse it. Be sure to include the handles in the machine-stitching. Finish the belt and add the closures and the pockets.

Alternatives. You could paint the pockets, embroider them, or make them of strong plain colors for children.

Illus. 138. Shield belt.

Materials. Heavy cottons, corduroys, wools, other heavy materials.

Color suggestions. Rainbow colors with black trimming.

Instructions. Make pattern for front piece and back, if desired. It might also be finished with just a collarband to hold it in place. Prepare stripes and cut pattern for required section. You can cut the stripes especially for each section, but it is easier to cut the pattern from the material. Sew one side, then the other and attach on the middle, making sure the seams are matched. Quilt or line as desired. Attach belt and line. Add closures.

Alternatives. Use metallics or embroider on stripes. Use the same material and make the pattern from embroidery or from the use of the quilting stitch. Use soft leather and topstitch. It could also be done, using the folding technique.

Illus. 139.
Patchwork shield belt.

Materials. Cottons or other heavy materials.

Color suggestions. I see it in primary colors—red and green or red and yellow—almost like a medieval shield.

Instructions. Make pattern for front piece and back if desired. It might also be finished with just a collarband to hold it in place. Prepare material and cut pattern from the material. If you prefer you could also form the pattern pieces to fit the pattern shape. Sew one side, then the other and attach, being careful to match the seams. Attach belt and closures. Quilt or line as desired. Attach backing or collar piece.

Alternatives. You could research the shield, which might represent your own family, or

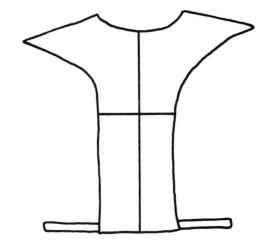

design your own shield. You could embroider names or flowers on the shield or you could use leather.

Illus. 140.
Appliquéd shield.

Materials. Lightweight cotton.

Color suggestions. Pastel shades of pink and light green.

Instructions. Make pattern for front piece and back if desired. It might be finished with a collarband or you could make a pattern for the back piece. Design patterns for flowers and leaves. Hem them and appliqué them onto background. Quilt or line the shield as desired. Attach belt and collar. Finish off piece by backing or quilting in the method described in the Basics chapter.

Alternatives. Paint on the design. Em-

broider the design instead of using appliqué. You could also machine-appliqué the pattern. You could use soft leather and topstitch it into place.

APPENDICES

Quilting
Stitches

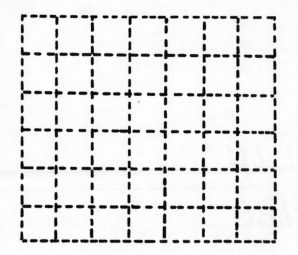

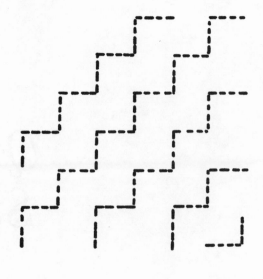

Embroidery
Stitches

Index